MASSAGE & OTHER PLAYS

First seen at the Lyric Theatre, Hammer
'startles with its compassion for two brui
touch borne out of meaning rather than n
molestation.' (Matt Wolf, *City Limits*)

In the same volume are two previously
and *Midnight Feast*.

MICHAEL WILCOX won the George Devine Award for Acco   3e
Theatre, Edinburgh, and Riverside Studios, London, 1981, and included in *Gay Plays: Volume One*). *Rents* (Traverse Theatre, 1979, and Lyric Theatre, Hammersmith, 1982) and *Lent* (Lyric Studio, Hammersmith, 1983) are also published by Methuen. *78 Revolutions* was premiered at the Traverse Theatre and the Lyric Studio in 1984. *Accounts* and *Lent* have both been filmed, and Wilcox won the Pye Television Award for Best Scripted Contribution to Television 1984-85 for the film version of *Lent* for BBC-TV.

The front cover shows David Allister as Dodge *and Dexter Fletcher as* Rikki *from the Lyric Hammersmith production of* Massage. *The photograph is reproduced by courtesy of Nobby Clarke.*

MASSAGE
& OTHER PLAYS

Massage
Dekka and Dava
Midnight Feast
by

MICHAEL WILCOX

A Methuen Paperback

British Library Cataloguing in Publication Data

Wilcox, Michael, 1943–
   Massage & Other Plays. — (A Methuen new theatrescript)
   I. Title
   822'.914   PR6073.I39/
   ISBN 0-413-16080-7

A METHUEN THEATRESCRIPT

First published as a paperback original in 1987
by Methuen London Ltd., 11 New Fetter Lane, London EC4P 4EE
and in the United States of America
by Methuen Inc., 29 West 35th Street, New York, NY 10001
Printed in Britain by Richard Clay Ltd, Bungay, Suffolk

Copyright © 1987 by Michael Wilcox

MASSAGE

Author's Note

Massage was written during the summer of 1986. I wrote it as part of a reaction to a series of frustrating experiences during the previous year. Discussions had been under way from the middle of 1985 with a West End management for a new play for the commercial (as opposed to subsidised) theatre, but the impresario concerned was taking an interminable time in sorting out the details of my contract. I was unwilling to write the new play until things were agreed between us and I knew precisely what was going to be involved. In the end, financial difficulties forced the management to withdraw from commissioning anything, and I was left high and dry. In 1985, BBC TV had to withdraw from a film project about the repatriation of German prisoners at the end of the Second World War (too costly), and the Oxford Playhouse withdrew from a play about Hector Berlioz (too large a cast), so a lot of hard work had been shelved. I was stuck in a very bad patch.

I phoned the Lyric, Hammersmith, and asked if they were interested in a single set, two or three character play for the Studio. Peter James, the artistic director of the Lyric, said he'd phone back in ten minutes, which he did. Yes, they'd like to commission a new play. *Massage* is the result.

I have often been asked to write a sequel to *Rents* which was set in Scotland in the mid-seventies. *Massage*, written eleven years later, is set in London in the mid-eighties. It also concerns a 'rent boy', but this time only one 'punter' is included. Ten years on, unemployment amongst the young has become a major problem in Britain. In *Rents*, one of the boys was a full-time student and the other worked in a shop, selling jeans. Rikki, in *Massage*, has taken advantage of a government scheme to learn his trade. If he wasn't making it as a 'rent boy', he'd probably be unemployed. Unlike the boys in *Rents*, he isn't homosexual either. He is fighting for his survival, making use of the resources he has to hand. His confrontation with a pederast, Tony Dodge, pulls into focus previous events in his life and his present vulnerability. Rikki's cocky self-assurance is very fragile. He is a distant cousin of those Brazilian street children, so brilliantly brought to the cinema screen in *Pixote*. As the gap between rich and poor gets wider in Britain, more and more young people will turn to thieving and prostitution to get by.

It seemed to me that there were three types of ending for the play. A catastrophic conclusion in which either Rikki or Dodge got murdered was a possibility, and I take the action right to the brink of such a disaster. These things do happen, but, mercifully, not that often. But murder would be too easy a conclusion and I didn't want to give anyone in the audience with a stoney heart and no compassion for either of the two main characters the satisfaction of seeing either wiped out in a blood bath. I could have opted for a cynical conclusion, in which Rikki picked up the bicycle and walked out with it. I find that ending credible also, but bleak and cold-hearted. The third option allows for the possibility of both men agreeing to meet up the following day. I do not regard this as a soft ending. They are not pedalling off into the sunset. Anyone who thinks this (and one or two critics did) hasn't been listening to the play. Rikki is still likely to get his treasured bicycle out of it, but there is no way he and Dodge are going to continue any sort of lasting relationship together. After a couple of trips on the bikes, Rikki's curiosity about Dodge will be more than satisfied, and Rikki will continue with his life as a massage boy. Dodge will depart on his trip round Britain. So the present ending seems to me to combine realism with a pinch of optimism.

One day, maybe I'll write a play with a catastrophic ending. I steered clear, deliberately, of catastrophe in *Rents*, *Accounts* and *Lent*, although I created the opportunities for mayhem in each play. *Massage* follows a similar pattern. Survival on this planet may indeed be under the severest threat, but amongst my characters, who may be considered politically insignificant by some, hope in some sort of tomorrow still exists.

Michael Wilcox, 1986

Massage was first performed at the Lyric Studio, Hammersmith on 6th October 1986 with the following cast:

RIKKI, *a massage boy*	Dexter Fletcher
DODGE, *a bicycle builder*	David Allister
JANE, *a journalist*	Pamela Merrick

Directed by Michael Wilcox
Designed by Bernard Culshaw
Lighting by John A. Williams
Company Manager Alex Reedijk
ASM Eleanor Aitken
DSM Paul Fryer

PART ONE

*Hammersmith, West London, 1986,
Wednesday 27th August, around
six o'clock. The back room of* TONY
DODGE's *bicycle shop. A work bench is
piled with toys and books belonging to
SIMON. A skateboard, with one set of
wheels removed, is held upside-down in a
vice. The frame of a new bicycle is held in
a jig. Its wheels are missing, but it is
otherwise complete. It has no toe clips.
Piles of rubbish and boxes of roughly
packed belongings are scattered around
the place.*

*A table has been laid for two. One door
leads to the main part of the shop and the
street entrance. Another door leads out of
the room into a small back kitchen. Parts
of bicycle frames, old wheels and various
debris of* DODGE's *trade litter the room.
There are piles of unopened letters.*
DODGE *is wearing a cyclist's tracksuit,
with cyclist's shorts, shirt and shoes.*

The telephone is ringing. TONY DODGE
*enters with his superb, fast-touring
bicycle. He has just dashed to the shops.
He props up the bicycle and goes to the
telephone just as it stops ringing. He
picks up his bicycle and hangs it by its
crossbar to a work frame, so that its
wheels are well clear of the ground. He
unpacks the small backpack and brings
out a bottle of fresh orange juice and a
box of cheap candles. He places two
candles in holders on the table. He fills
an empty jug full of the orange juice. He
hides his wallet in its usual hiding-place
above one of the work benches. The shop
door bell rings.*

RIKKI *has walked through the shop to
the back room. He comes to the door of
the back room. He is nineteen from East
London, but looks younger. He has a
shoulder bag with his things in it. He has
never visited* DODGE *before.*

RIKKI: Mr Dodge?

DODGE: Come in.

RIKKI: I'm the massage.

DODGE: Oh. Good. Everything's ready.

RIKKI *is surprised and fascinated by
the state of the room.*

DODGE: I did explain to your boss.

RIKKI: What?

DODGE: What's your name?

RIKKI: Rikki.

DODGE: Where are you from?

RIKKI: Upton Park.

DODGE: West Ham supporter?

RIKKI: Yes.

DODGE: Never mind.

RIKKI: Where do you want it?
    The massage, Mr Dodge. In here? In
    the bedroom?

DODGE: Not yet.

RIKKI: I've only got half-an-hour.

DODGE: Have you eaten?

RIKKI: Yes.

DODGE: When?

RIKKI: Lunch-time.

DODGE: I want you to eat with me.

RIKKI: Eat what?

DODGE: You'll see.

RIKKI: You some sort of creep?

DODGE: Watch it!

RIKKI: What do you want?

DODGE: I've done a meal. I want
    someone to share it. Right?

RIKKI: Is that what you're paying for?

DODGE: That's between me and your
    boss.

RIKKI: Know him, do you?

DODGE: Done business.

RIKKI: I mean personally.

DODGE: Too many questions.

RIKKI: Sorry.

DODGE: You staying or leaving?

RIKKI: Staying.

DODGE: Sit down then.

RIKKI: Here?

DODGE: Yes.

    RIKKI *sits at the table.*

DODGE (*tossing a box of matches at* RIKKI): Light the candles.

RIKKI *lights the candles.*

RIKKI: Where's the menu, Mr Dodge?

DODGE *goes into the kitchen to fetch the first course. As soon as he's out of the room,* RIKKI *gets up and looks at* DODGE's *superb bicycle. He gets back to his seat before* DODGE *enters with two bowls of soup.*

RIKKI: Tomato! My mum does that!

RIKKI *starts to drink the soup.* DODGE *looks at him disapprovingly and offers* RIKKI *a serviette.* RIKKI *lays down his spoon, getting the message.*

RIKKI: Sorry, Mr Dodge. Do you want me to say Grace or something?

DODGE: That won't be necessary.

RIKKI: You sound like a teacher at school. When he was on dinner duty, he used to say something in Latin or Greek . . . like he was casting a spell over the food. We used to call him Caligula . . . you know . . . after the video.

DODGE *picks up a sharp bread knife and starts to cut a slice of bread.*

DODGE: Bread?

RIKKI: Just a bit.

DODGE *passes* RIKKI *a slice on the point of the knife.*

RIKKI: Sharp knife, Mr Dodge. Can I start? It's getting cold.

DODGE: Yes.

They both eat their soup.

RIKKI: What's all this, then? Your birthday?

DODGE: Not mine.

RIKKI: Someone else's?

DODGE: Do you have to ask questions?

RIKKI: Sorry. Only asking, Mr Dodge.

DODGE: How old are you?

RIKKI: Twenty-two . . . that's what I told the boss.

DODGE: Seventeen . . . sixteen . . .?

RIKKI: Leave off! I'm legal.

DODGE: Do you read?

RIKKI: Books?

DODGE: Yes.

RIKKI: No. Once read a book about sea fishing. I can read.

DODGE: Newspapers?

RIKKI: Sometimes. Don't waste my money. I read other people's.

DODGE: Not interested in the news, then?

RIKKI: You want to watch the tele?

DODGE: No I don't.

RIKKI: Do what you want, Mr Dodge.

DODGE *clears away the soup plates and takes them to the kitchen. As soon as he has left the room,* RIKKI *gets up and searches through the shelves above the work-bench. He finds a pair of cyclist's gloves and pockets them. He also finds* DODGE's *wallet, opens it and sees that there's about £30 in it. He hears* DODGE *coming back and stuffs the wallet back in its hiding place without taking any of the money. He sits down as* DODGE *enters with a covered dish and a plate of sausage rolls.*

RIKKI: Great! Sausage rolls! Obviously a daring cook, Mr Dodge!

DODGE: Don't touch.

DODGE *goes to fetch the plates.* RIKKI *immediately tries to lift the lid off the covered dish and burns his fingers.* DODGE *returns with the plates and starts to serve.*

DODGE: Two?

RIKKI: Yes.

DODGE *passes* RIKKI *the plate and, with a cloth, takes the lid off the covered dish.*

RIKKI: Beans! Murder!

RIKKI *takes a few spoonfuls of beans.*

RIKKI (*singing*): 'Happy birthday to you . . . Happy birthday . . .'

DODGE (*silencing him*): Thank you, Rikki!

RIKKI: Sorry, Mr Dodge. Who is it, then?

DODGE: I'm not talking about it.

RIKKI: Oh come on, sir!

DODGE: Why call me sir?

RIKKI: Good manners, isn't it? You're like that, sir, aren't you? Go on, sir. Tell us, sir. Oh go on, sir.

DODGE: Just a kid I know.

RIKKI: His birthday, is it?

DODGE: Yes.

RIKKI: Your boyfriend, is he?

DODGE: Shut up!

RIKKI: Only asking.

They carry on eating.

Your lover?

DODGE: I'm not gay.

RIKKI: Bloody hell!

DODGE: You make so many assumptions.

RIKKI: Oh God . . .

DODGE: You think we're all like you!

RIKKI: Here! Leave me out of it, right? I'm doing my job, aren't I!

DODGE: He was my companion.

RIKKI: Oh yes . . . I've heard of them.

DODGE: Just eat.

RIKKI: Tell me if you want. I have to listen to all sorts of stuff.

DODGE: This is his favourite meal. He was supposed to be here.

DODGE *takes another mouthful of sausage roll.*

RIKKI: *Bon appetit*, Mr Dodge.

DODGE: I didn't want to eat alone. Phoned the agency. Yours all right?

RIKKI (*pushing his plate away*): Memorable.

DODGE *takes the plates. RIKKI gets up.*

DODGE: Sit down! There's more to come.

RIKKI *looks at the half-built bicycle in the jig.*
DODGE *returns with some jelly out of a jelly mould.*
RIKKI *laughs when he sees what's next.*

DODGE: This is a bloody mistake.

RIKKI: Looks OK to me.

DODGE *serves out some jelly onto* RIKKI's *plate.*

Any cream?

DODGE *passes a jug of cream.* RIKKI *helps himself.*

DODGE: I shouldn't have called you.

RIKKI: Don't say that, Mr Dodge. I'm really enjoying this. Excellent jelly, Mr Dodge!

RIKKI *eats the jelly with enthusiasm.*

DODGE: Why do you eat so fast?

RIKKI: Brought up in a Children's Home. If you didn't eat fast you didn't get seconds.
Interested in football?

DODGE: I used to take Simon to see Chelsea.

RIKKI: Chelsea!

DODGE: I suppose that was the start of it.

RIKKI: Met him in the Shed?

DODGE: I knew him before that. I knew his mother.

RIKKI: So he's called Simon, is he?

DODGE: Don't talk about him.

RIKKI: What do you want to go to Chelsea for? They're a bunch of wimps!

DODGE: He wanted to go.

RIKKI: Blimey! You've got problems there, mate! Did his mother come with you?

DODGE: Of course not.

RIKKI: But you said you knew her. Shag me, love my son? That sort of game, was it?

DODGE: Fuck off!

DODGE *grabs the plates and takes them off into the kitchen.*
RIKKI *explores* SIMON's *toys.*
DODGE *returns with a birthday cake with the candles lit. There are only twelve candles on the cake.* DODGE *turns off the lights, although it is still light outside. He places the cake in front of* RIKKI *on the table.* RIKKI *is about to blow out the candles.*

DODGE: Make a wish.

RIKKI *makes a wish.*

RIKKI: Not telling you, mind.

RIKKI *blows out all the candles and also the two other candles on the table for good measure. DODGE is irritated by this and he goes to turn on the light again. RIKKI stares at the candles on the cake.*

RIKKI: Jesus! Twelve candles, Mr Dodge?

DODGE: You can count too!

RIKKI: Your lover . . . sorry . . . companion . . . nice boy was he? Pretty? What a fucking mess!

DODGE: Glass of orange?

RIKKI: Do us a favour!

DODGE *pours out a full glass of orange juice and plants it in front of RIKKI.*

DODGE: Drink it!

RIKKI *sniffs it suspiciously, takes a sip, then downs the whole lot defiantly.*

DODGE: Good boy.

DODGE *picks up the sharp knife and holds it in front of RIKKI.*

DODGE: Now cut the cake! ✓

RIKKI *doesn't move. He's worried by DODGE's aggression.*

DODGE: I said cut it!

RIKKI *takes the knife and insolently removes the twelve candles from the cake before holding the knife poised above the cake.*

DODGE: Make another wish!

RIKKI *looks at the half-built bicycle and makes another wish. Then he cuts the cake roughly and deposits a slice on DODGE's plate. He takes a small bit for himself and nibbles it.*

DODGE: Not bad, is it?

RIKKI: Lovely.

DODGE: How long are you staying?

RIKKI: Not long.

DODGE: Another twenty minutes?

RIKKI: Can I phone the boss?

DODGE: Sure.

RIKKI *goes to the phone and dials the agency.*

RIKKI: Hi . . . Rikki . . . anything else tonight?
I'm still in Hammersmith.
Yes . . . OK . . . he's a food fetishist.
Where's that?
(*to DODGE*): Pen? (DODGE *indicates where a biro and pad are kept.*)
OK . . . I got that. What time? Right.
You got this number?
Right.
Cash, credit card or account?
Cheers.
Bye . .

RIKKI *hangs up.*

RIKKI: Got another job.

DODGE: Haven't had my time yet.

RIKKI: Had the meal, haven't I?

DODGE: I'm paying for this.

RIKKI: Offered you a massage.

DODGE: Stay a bit longer.

RIKKI: Why?

DODGE: Company.

RIKKI: Nothing queer.

DODGE: No.

RIKKI: OK.

DODGE: Where's the next job?

RIKKI: Not far. Round the corner.

DODGE: Finish your cake.

RIKKI: No.

DODGE: OK was it?

RIKKI: Lovely, Mr Dodge.

DODGE: Bought it at Safeways. Did the icing myself.

RIKKI: Tell me about your bikes.

DODGE: Actually, I'm a bike fetishist.

RIKKI: Your shop, is it?

DODGE: Used to be. Gone out of business.

RIKKI: Bust?

DODGE: More or less.

RIKKI: Somebody screwed you?

DODGE: I'm a craftsman.

RIKKI: Really?

DODGE: Halfords finished me. Flashy metal off the peg. That's where the money is.

RIKKI: Start selling flashy metal.

DODGE: Can't make a living mending spokes. Got to sell bikes to survive.

RIKKI: Custom-built stuff?

DODGE: You into bikes?

RIKKI: Don't mind them.

DODGE: What have you got?

RIKKI: A Raleigh. Too small for me now. Still use it sometimes. I used to love my bike. What's special about yours?

DODGE (*indicating his own fast tourer that's hanging up*): This one?

RIKKI: Yes.

DODGE *fetches it down and places it in front of* RIKKI.

DODGE: Good frame. Reynolds 531 fork blades and stays. Butted frame tubes. Cyclone sealed bearing hubs. Suntour ARX derailler. Weinmann brakes. Campagnolo headset. Brilliant!

(*Vary this description to suit the particular bicycle used in production.*)

Built the wheels myself, of course.

RIKKI: Build wheels, do you?

DODGE: Vital part.

RIKKI (*while* DODGE *is replacing bike on its hanging frame*): Always had trouble with wheels. Out of shape. Ping! Another spoke gone. Used to fiddle on with one of them spoke key things.

DODGE: Making matters worse.

RIKKI: Never could figure them out.

DODGE: Off the peg jobs . . . some of the frames are OK. Lousy wheels. Get you out of the shop.

RIKKI (*picking up one of* DODGE's *wheels*): This one of yours?

DODGE: Yes.

RIKKI: You built this from scratch?

DODGE: Yes.

RIKKI: Really lasts, does it?

DODGE: Yes.

RIKKI: Cost a bomb?

DODGE: More to start with. Less in the long run.

RIKKI: What's the difference?

DODGE: Quality parts. No one wants quality these days. A few enthusiasts, maybe. They do their own repairs when something happens. Get the parts off me. Don't blame them. That's what I'd do.

RIKKI: So what happened?

DODGE: Got into a tangle with the VAT. Bastards on the Council stuck up the Rates.

RIKKI: So you cut your losses and quit.

DODGE: Quality doesn't pay. Trash rules.

RIKKI: Could you fix my bike?

DODGE: Could do.

RIKKI: Selling off some of your wheels cheap?

DODGE: Hold on.

DODGE *fetches a tape measure and measures* RIKKI's *inside leg.*

DODGE: You need a 22-inch frame. (*This depends on the height of the actor.*) I might be able to help you.

RIKKI: I've got no money.

DODGE: Liar.

RIKKI: Well, got some.

DODGE: Stacks with what you're up to.

RIKKI: The boss collects the money. I just get a percentage. A few tips. I'm doing all right.

DODGE: You a good masseur?

RIKKI: Brilliant. Got magic fingers.

DODGE: Practise on yourself, do you?

RIKKI: Shut your face. I'm trained. Qualified.

DODGE: Where did you go? Oxford?

RIKKI: I went on a government scheme. I'm a success story.

DODGE: What sort of scheme's that, then?

RIKKI; I was your unemployed youth. they sent me to the swimming baths. They've got this Turkish suite, and this old geezer . . . all covered in tattoos and hairless . . . he did the massage. He showed me what to do and the punters liked being done by a young lad. When my time was up, they never kept me on. Said they were sorry, but they hadn't got the money. Saw this ad. for a masseur. Followed it up. Said I was twenty-two. Got the job, didn't I. Been at it for three months now. So, thanks to Maggie, I'm a successful, qualified, upwardly mobile rent boy!

DODGE: While I'm in the shit!

RIKKI: Yes. Have you got any of those sexy, one-piece racing outfits?

DODGE *rummages around in one of his boxes and finds one. He throws it over to* RIKKI.

RIKKI: Thanks, Mr Dodge!

DODGE: Tony.

RIKKI (*Putting away the suit in his shoulder bag*): Tony. How did you get mixed up with this kid?

DODGE: Big mistake.

RIKKI: You don't look the sort to me.

DODGE: What does 'the sort' look like?

RIKKI: Not saying. Don't look like one, that's all.

DODGE: You know about these things, do you?

RIKKI: Not saying.

DODGE: Ah . . .

RIKKI: What happened?

DODGE: Met him and his mum in Benidorm. Me and his mum, we got on together. She's bright. Journalist. Freelance.

RIKKI: You screw her?

DODGE: Shut it!

RIKKI: Just asking. Get on with it. Go on!

DODGE: We got on together. Good couple of weeks. You been there?

RIKKI: I haven't been anywhere. Except Southend.

DODGE: We got home, carried on. Used to see her two or three times a week. Used to cook for each other. You know . . . company. Simon was crackers on

bikes. His mum used to park him here. Took him to the cinema. Bike trips. Camping.

RIKKI: Great.

DODGE: Appeals to you, does it?

RIKKI: Not half!

DODGE: We were away in Dorset.

RIKKI: You and the kid.

DODGE: Yes. Weekend trip. Out all day. Really tired. Got the tent up. Cooked a meal.

RIKKI:,Beans!

DODGE: Got on great.

RIKKI: Is that it?

DODGE: Just about.

RIKKI: How old was he?

DODGE: Just a kid.

RIKKI: Ten? Nine?

DODGE: Suppose so.

RIKKI: Fucked him, did you?

DODGE *is enraged by this. He walks over to* RIKKI's *shoulder bag, picks it up and throws it at him.*

DODGE: Fuck off out of here!

RIKKI: Fucked the kid! Is that it?

DODGE *grabs* RIKKI *and tries to hustle him out of the door.*
RIKKI *surprises him with a hip throw and* DODGE *suddenly ends up on his back on the floor.*

DODGE: Jesus Christ!

RIKKI: Neat!

DODGE: Fucking twat!

RIKKI: Did judo at evening classes. Free with a UB40! Not bad, eh?

DODGE (*more stunned than injured*): You've just broken my fucking back!

RIKKI: Sorry, Mr Dodge . . . Tony . . . sir. Let's have a look.

As RIKKI *tries to touch him,* DODGE *recoils, as though unwilling to be touched.*

RIKKI: Steady. Let's see. It was a perfectly reasonable question. No need to fly off the handle. Sit still. That's better. I won't hurt you. Honest.

DODGE *calms down, but is still unwilling to be touched.*

So there's you and this kid. Tell us, Tony. I want to know. Please.

DODGE: He just . . . kind of . . . flung his arms around me.

RIKKI: Little Simon?

DODGE: . . . hung onto me as though I was the last driftwood in a big ocean. We never did anything really heavy together.

RIKKI: What did you do?

DODGE: Ohhh . . . he just got curious about my body . . . about his . . . how things worked. I never . . . Christ no! All over in a moment. We . . .

RIKKI: What?

DODGE: . . . we were lying there . . . him playing with me . . .

RIKKI: . . . starkers . . .

DODGE: . . . and I just came off. Bang! That was that. Dodge the child-molester. Didn't seem such a big deal at the time.

RIKKI: You OK?

DODGE: Yes. I think so. Fallen off the bike enough times.

RIKKI: Thought you were an expert.

DODGE: Simon thought it was fantastic.

RIKKI: A new toy. So what have you done with him?

DODGE: Last night his mother caught him playing with himself in the bath. They had a row. She's become jealous of me. My 'influence'.

RIKKI: Still take her out?

DODGE: Not any more.

RIKKI: Packed her in?

DODGE: Got too involved. Too complicated. Didn't want to move in with them.

RIKKI: So you was screwing her and her son?

DODGE: Wasn't like that exactly.

RIKKI: Has she found out?

DODGE: I don't think so. I thought I'd give Simon a birthday treat. But she thumps her fist down and says 'No way!' He's got his own mates. You know . . . his own age. Always been his own boss as far as I was concerned.

RIKKI: This would look bad on the front page of the *News of the World*.

DODGE: It would. It seemed natural at the time. A bit odd, really. But there we are.

DODGE *goes to the telephone.*

I've got to call him. I'm sure he was trying to contact me earlier.

He dials.

Do you mind?

RIKKI: Go ahead.

DODGE: Simon . . . mum's out is she? Good. Yes, I'm sorry too. What are you doing?

(*To* RIKKI): He's watching *The Blue Lagoon*!
Good is it? No idiot! Brook Shields isn't being attacked by piranahs! Wait and see. Ask your mother. No! She'll explain. No!
Do you want to go camping with the cubs? Yes . . . you'll have a great time. Well . . . the bike'll be there when you get back.
Look . . . sorry it's been such a mess today. Happy Birthday. Just do what she says. Give it time. Have you said anything?
Good.
I'll be off on my trip.
Of course I'll send you a card. I'll send you loads!
Done your homework? Well get on with it! Watch the video later, then! No, I won't tell her.
OK . . . sorry to interrupt.
'Bye.

SIMON *has hung up on him.*
DODGE *replaces the receiver.*

RIKKI: What's the trip?

DODGE: I'm going to cycle round Britain.

RIKKI: What, right round?

DODGE: Yes.

RIKKI: Which way?

DODGE (*making a clockwise motion*): That way.

RIKKI (*imitating him*): That way?

DODGE: Yes.

RIKKI: Clockwise.

DODGE: Yes.

RIKKI: Why?

DODGE: If I head northwards up the West coast, I'll have the wind behind me.

RIKKI: You're mental.

DODGE: I've got to get away.

RIKKI: Have you sold this place?

DODGE: I quit the lot next week.

RIKKI: Where are you going to live?

DODGE: Going to store what's left of my stuff in a garage. Then off on my bike with my tent and get the hell out of it!

RIKKI: Running away.

DODGE: Dead right.

RIKKI: What from?

DODGE: This bloody city.

RIKKI: It's OK.

DODGE: Owning things. Bills, taxes, rates . . .

DODGE *scatters handfuls of letters, all unopened.*

RIKKI: You're daft. You might have won the pools.

DODGE: Don't do them.

RIKKI: No one ever writes to me.

DODGE: Somewhere out there, I'm filed on a dozen computers. I've got a shop so they think I've got money.

RIKKI: So you'd rather be a tramp?

DODGE: There's still some cash left.

RIKKI *goes over to where* DODGE's *wallet is hidden and fetches it out so that* DODGE *can see him.*

RIKKI: If it'll make you feel better, you can give all your money to me.

RIKKI *puts the wallet back again.*

DODGE: I'm not giving it away to anyone. That's why I don't open letters.

RIKKI *is fascinated by* DODGE's *brilliant bicycle.*

DODGE: Riding a bike's like flying. You know those dreams you sometimes have, when you kick your legs and take off? And you say: 'Look at me! Flying's easy! Come on! Just try it!' And you wonder why you haven't been picked for the Olympic games when you can clear a hundred metres at a single leap. When you're sailing down a long hill, and the bike is perfectly balanced and silent, and you look ahead, you might as well be flying under your own power. And you can hear and smell the countryside on a bike, and feel the pockets of warm and cold air sail past you as you go. There's nothing like it, Rikki.

RIKKI: What are you going to live on? Hedgehogs?

DODGE: I told you. I've got some money. Not much else.
So you were in a Children's Home?

RIKKI: Yes. 'Till I was ten.

DODGE: What was that like?

RIKKI: OK, I suppose. You don't know any different, do you . . . You think about having a mum and dad like normal kids at school, but then you have your treats, like going to the pantomime or the cinema. And you're there with all your mates. And you think kids with families are probably having the hell kicked out of them. You're better off with what you know sometimes. I was adopted, mind. I've got a mum now.

DODGE: When did you get a mum?

RIKKI: When I was ten. The people there, they got me all dressed up 'cause I was going to meet some one who wanted to adopt me. That's what the kids there dreamed of. Some one coming. Some one good . . . you know . . . to take you with them . . . to be your dad . . . take you on holidays and that . . . have your own room and your own things . . . possessions. Anyway, I was in this room and the door opened and this man and woman walked in, and I remember thinking, 'Bloody Hell! I'm not going off with them! The other kids'll think I'm daft!' But I did. Just for the afternoon. You don't clear off for good, just like that. They have to get to know you, to see if they like you.

DODGE: Where did they take you?

RIKKI: First time out?

DODGE: Yes.

RIKKI: Caught the train to Southend.

DODGE: What did you do?

RIKKI: I'd been there before with the other kids . . . you know . . . from the Home. Seen the Wax Works. 'Torture through the Ages.' Not much cop. Supposed to be educational. Looked at the *Golden Hind*. Went on the racing cars by the pier. Great to be with someone with money to spend. When we was having a day out with the Home, we had to spend a lot of time just watching other kids having fun. Then we went to the Kursaal . . . big dippers and that. But we was running out of money. There was this incredible ride called The Toboggan. So mum and dad and me gets on this sledge thing and start to get hoisted up to the top of the Cresta Run. And once you're on it, there's no escape, even if you have a heart attack on the way up. Cause you can't see, when you pays your money, just how steep it is 'cause it goes right out of sight. But on the way up me mum starts screaming and dad's had a few drinks and says he feels sick and I was laughing. And when we gets to the top there's this lad with tattoos like a gipsy and he doesn't take the blindest notice of me dad, who threatens to bottle him. And the next thing we know, we're charging down this vertical run on a wooden tray at a hundred miles an hour. And we all screamed our heads off. And when we got to the top of the next hump, dad threw up and mum lost her hat! And I thought, 'If they can do this for me, maybe they're not so daft.'

DODGE: Still living with them?

RIKKI: Live with me mum.

DODGE: What about your dad?

RIKKI: Dropped dead! In the front hall. Been on the booze. Boing! Dead!

DODGE: When was that?

RIKKI: A few years back. Thought of killing him myself. Did it for me, didn't he!

DODGE: What did you want to kill him for?

RIKKI: This and that.

DODGE: Tell me.

RIKKI: No.

DODGE: Private?

RIKKI: Yes.

DODGE: What are your ambitions?

RIKKI: Me?

DODGE: Yes.

RIKKI: Get some money. Get married. Have kids. Buy a Volvo. A place in Barking.

DODGE: Is that it?

RIKKI: Yes.

DODGE: I thought you weren't interested in girls.

RIKKI: Thought wrong, didn't you.

DODGE: I suppose I did.

RIKKI: I do this massage job 'cause I like it and it makes me money. I love kids. I'm going to have a big family one day. And when I do, I'm going to love them. Going to play with them. Take them to the football. Trips to the seaside. See films together. Do something special at Christmas and birthdays. See these hands?

DODGE: Yes.

RIKKI: There was a lot of hate in them once, but it's going away. They've handled so many bodies, you wouldn't believe it. Old ones, young ones, fat and skinny ones, queer and fucking queer! And it's made me strong. Look at my muscles! A lot of hate's gone out of me. Done me good, this job. My mum's proud of me. I buy her presents. Look after her.

DODGE: Got a girl friend?

RIKKI: Got a few.

DODGE: Anyone special?

RIKKI: No. Got to find the right one for my kids, haven't I?

DODGE: You'll have beautiful boys.

RIKKI: I think so. And if anyone got their hands on them, I'd kill them.

DODGE: I think you'd better go now.

RIKKI: What's the time?

RIKKI *grabs* DODGE*'s wrist and twists it to look at his watch.*

Still got a minute or two.

DODGE: Do you want me to fix your bike, then?

RIKKI: Got enough bits?

DODGE: Yes.

RIKKI (*admiring the half-built bicycle*): I like travel. Fancy a trip to Southend?

DODGE: On the bikes?

RIKKI: If you want.

DODGE: Better places to go than that.

RIKKI: Is there?

DODGE: Too many cars.

RIKKI: Where's Dorset? Is it far?

DODGE: Quite far.

RIKKI: Is it good?

DODGE: Very good.

RIKKI: What's there?

DODGE: Country. Cliffs. The sea. Better than Southend.

RIKKI: Seen the sea.

DODGE: It's different. Depends where you go.

RIKKI: Suppose so.

DODGE: What do you want to fix up?

RIKKI: Are you stopping in tonight?

DODGE: Yes. Going to work on the bike.

RIKKI (*gazing at the half-built bike*): Reynolds 531?

DODGE: Yes.

RIKKI: What size?

DODGE: 22-inch frame. (*This size depends on the height of the actor playing* RIKKI.)

RIKKI: Got wheels, has it?

DODGE: They're in the shop.

RIKKI: Look. I'm only going round the corner for the next 'un. Can I call back in on my way home?

DODGE: OK.

RIKKI: Where's that racing outfit you give us? Oh yea, in the bag. This is going to make someone happy tonight! I'm wicked!

DODGE: What do you mean 'wicked'?

RIKKI: Oh . . . you know . . . not really.

DODGE: Am I wicked?

RIKKI: Definitely.

DODGE: I don't think so.

RIKKI: Not all the time, maybe.

DODGE: When?

RIKKI: Not when you're on the bike. With the kid you are.

DODGE: It was an accident.

RIKKI: Not after the first time.

DODGE: Who said it happened again?

RIKKI: 'course it did! You done him, Mr Dodge. That's a fact. And you shouldn't of.

DODGE: You know fuck all.

RIKKI: That's what you think.

DODGE: He calls the tune.

RIKKI: He shouldn't.

DODGE: Why?

RIKKI: You shouldn't let him.

DODGE: Why?

RIKKI: You're grown-up. He isn't.

DODGE: He is grown-up. In his way he is.

RIKKI: You were like his dad, with his mum and that. Dads shouldn't do things like that. Dads are for other things.

DODGE: What do you know about it?

RIKKI: Plenty.

DODGE: Like what?

RIKKI: Not saying.

DODGE: Something happened to you? This Children's Home, queer was it?

RIKKI: It was OK. It was good really. Saved my life. I think they did. Good people, Mr Dodge. Didn't agree with all of it. Too much God, not enough food. They weren't perfect. But they weren't bad either.

DODGE: Not quite what I asked.

RIKKI: You was after dirty stories. I'm not telling none. Boys being boys is one thing. Grown ups being boys is a pain in the arse! You don't need dirty stories from me. You've got your own, haven't you!

The bell in the front of the shop sounds.

DODGE: Hang on.

JANE *has walked through the shop to the backroom and enters. She is carrying a shoulder bag of her own and a bag full of* DODGE's *clothes that she has washed and ironed. She is surprised to see* RIKKI *and wonders who he is.*

JANE: Oh! I didn't know you had company.

RIKKI: Sorry.

JANE: Who's your friend, Tony?

RIKKI: I'm just going, Mr Dodge.

JANE: Don't rush off just because I've come. Here are your things, Tony. (*To* RIKKI) I do all this for him. Crazy, don't you think?

DODGE: Thanks.

JANE: What's your name?

RIKKI: I'm nobody.

JANE: Tell me.

RIKKI: Rikki, Mrs . . .

DODGE: I think Rikki has another appointment.

RIKKI: Yes.

JANE: Visiting are you?

RIKKI: Got to dash!

RIKKI *goes to pick up his bag.*

JANE: Wait! Oh look! All Simon's toys. And some of his books! That's where they got to! Well! I don't think you'll be needing these here any longer. Rikki, be an angel and carry this lot out to my car. Hold on! Where's a box? You don't mind me using one of yours, Tony?

She fetches one of Tony's boxes and empties out the contents. Then she holds the empty box in RIKKI's *direction.* RIKKI *doesn't move. He looks at* DODGE *for his approval.*

RIKKI: Mr Dodge?

DODGE: Do what she says.

RIKKI *grabs the box from* JANE *rudely, and starts to fill it with Simon's things.*

JANE: Is the skateboard mended yet? Simon was very anxious about that.

DODGE: Haven't had time.

JANE: Oh well! He'll have to go without!

JANE *takes the skateboard out of the vice.*

RIKKI: Leave it, Mrs . . . It's no good with the wheels in bits. Tony'll mend it. He's clever, him.

JANE: I know. Do you want it? Take it.

RIKKI: No! Look! He's good with wheels, aren't you, Tony.

JANE: What do you want to take things apart for? This was OK the last time I saw it.

DODGE: I was servicing the bearings.

JANE: It's just a toy, for God's sake!

RIKKI *takes the skateboard.*

RIKKI: You don't understand nothing! There's lots of little steel balls inside there. They get full of dirt and stuff so they don't do their job proper. Clean them. Oil them. And they don't half go! That's right, ain't it, Tony?

DODGE: Exactly right.

JANE *is stuffing things into the box without paying much attention.* RIKKI *is getting angry about this.*

RIKKI: Oy! Mrs! Look at these!

RIKKI *goes over to* DODGE's *fast-touring bicycle that is hanging up, he turns the pedal and sets the rear wheel spinning furiously.*

Tony made them! Perfect! All them little balls doing their job. One action and things are set spinning for ages. That's my energy you're looking at. Still going, ain't it? Long after what I've done. That machine, it's just

waiting for some one to make it come
to life.

RIKKI *goes to the box of toys while
the wheel goes on spinning.*

Now where do you want me to stuff
this?

JANE: By the shop door.

RIKKI: Right, Mrs . . . Tony'll fix it . . .
the skateboard!

RIKKI *leaves with his bag and
the box.*

JANE: OK. We've got to talk.

DODGE: Well?

JANE: Fetch me a coffee.

DODGE *walks off into the kitchen,
shutting the door loudly. JANE
immediately gets a 'Walkman' tape
recorder out of her bag and sets it
going. She records herself.*

JANE: Tony Dodge's place . . .
Wednesday 27th August . . . (*She
looks at her watch.*) . . . 6.47 pm . . .

*She then conceals the tape recorder,
which is still recording, in her bag,
making sure that the built-in
microphone will pick up the following
conversation. She sets it down on the
table in front of her and awaits
DODGE's return with the coffee.*

PART TWO

JANE *is still sitting at the table as at the end of* Part One.
DODGE *brings in two cups of coffee. He sets them down on the table, where* JANE *is sitting, and moves her handbag out of the way.* JANE *conceals her concern about the new positioning of the tape recorder.* DODGE *sits with her at the table.*

JANE: Has Simon phoned?

DODGE: No.

JANE: Good.

DODGE: Thanks for doing these.
(*Meaning the washing*).

JANE: That's the last.

DODGE: Right.

JANE: When are you leaving?

DODGE: Next week. You know that.

JANE: Just making sure.

DODGE: Then you'll be rid of me.

JANE: Are you planning to write to Simon?

DODGE: Yes.

JANE: Don't.

DODGE: You can't stop me.

JANE: Don't try it.

DODGE: He's looking forward to postcards from all over the place. What's up with you, then? Two days ago you were all keen for this party. I get everything ready. Then 'He's not coming, you bastard. You'll never see him again!' And all that crap. What the hell's going on?

JANE: I went into the bathroom and he started screaming at me to get out. He's never done that before.

DODGE: Growing up, isn't he.

JANE: We were talking later and he tried to explain. You came up. I guessed the rest.

DODGE: Guessed what?

JANE: What have you done?

DODGE: Nothing.

JANE: I'm his mother. I've got a right to know the truth. There's no one else here. Just you and me. Now tell me.

DODGE: There's nothing to tell.

JANE: That won't do.

DODGE: You've dumped him on me for the past three years, while you fly about writing trashy stories . . .

JANE: Rubbish.

DODGE: All you've ever done is work out how to get him out of the way.

JANE: You think so?

DODGE: Yes.

JANE: You think bringing up a boy on your own is easy?

DODGE: No.

JANE: I have to earn money. I've got a good job. Unsocial hours. Of course there are problems when he's not at school. What am I supposed to do? Pack my job in?

DODGE: Possibly.

JANE: Thanks a lot.

DODGE: What did you do? You sent him round here. 'Go and see Tony'. 'Tony, can he come and have tea with you? I'm out on a job.' So I more or less adopt him.

JANE: You didn't mind.

DODGE: Of course I didn't. I love him. Great kid. And now you swing your bloody great axe on us! Talk about everything happening at once. I've lost everything now, haven't I. The shop's not your fault. After all I've done! And there was us, remember?

JANE: Don't.

DODGE: We were doing OK.

JANE: That's finished.

DODGE: Why?

JANE: I'm not going through all that.

DODGE: There was no one else. For a year. I was happy. So were you. Then . . . finish . . . go home . . . you're not staying. A week later . . . let's go to a film . . . come round for a meal . . .

JANE: What have you done to my son?

DODGE: Been like a father. You're

jealous, aren't you! First it was 'Love me, love my son'. Now it's 'Hands off the pair of us!' But you're two separate people, aren't you? He's got his life, you've got yours.

JANE: I'll go to the police if I have to.

DODGE: What?

JANE: He's only twelve years old. I'm not bluffing. You've been at him, haven't you!

DODGE: What are you getting at?

JANE: You bloody well know!

DODGE: I'm the best friend he ever had.

JANE: Do you want the police round here?

DODGE: Of course not.

JANE: You've been screwing Simon.

DODGE: You're fucking mental!

JANE: I'll prove it. I'll take him to a doctor. No. The police will do that.

DODGE: How can you think of doing that? To your own son!

JANE: Tell me now. Just the two of us.

DODGE: I haven't been screwing anyone. You were the last, damn it!

JANE: The doctor should be able to tell me.

DODGE: Are you seriously going to let some guy stick his fingers into Simon? Humiliate him? Just to satisfy some crazy idea of yours?

JANE: If you've given him some sort of disease, we need to know.

DODGE: Jesus Christ! I haven't done anything like that! It's all in your head!

JANE: What have you done?

DODGE: Pack it in!

JANE: You've put your arms round him. Cuddled him.

DODGE: Of course I have. You've seen us together. You never objected.

JANE: I don't mean when I've been there. I mean when you go off camping. On holiday together. You've been very close, haven't you?

DODGE: Yes.

JANE: He's told me how you've cuddled

him naked. How he's touched you.

DODGE: Of course we undress. How do you suppose we keep clean? Look! What is this?

JANE: Interested, isn't he?

DODGE: What in?

JANE: Things.

DODGE: Normal kid.

JANE: Used to be.

DODGE: Christ!

JANE: You just got carried away?

DODGE: Shit!

JANE: I can understand. Just tell me, Tony.

DODGE: For fuck's sake!

JANE: It isn't fair. After everything. Fucking tell me! OK . . . you've been naked together.

DODGE: So what?

JANE: He's told me, Tony. 'Mummy, he's all stiff down here.' How you've got him to wank you off!
Let's both be adult about this, shall we? How often has this happened? Either you or him?

DODGE: Shut your fucking face!

JANE: Do you want me to bring Simon round here? I mean it! I will! I'll get him to repeat everything he's told me!

DODGE: I don't believe you.

JANE: Just try me! Let's get this out of the way now. Together. Privately.

DODGE: Once or twice.

JANE: How often?

DODGE: Just a few times. There was nothing bad about it. He was curious. Interested. You said so yourself. That's all there was to it.

JANE: Did he suck you off?

DODGE: Will you fuck off, you bloody woman! He was curious about what he had between his legs. Boys are like that!

JANE: You know all about boys, do you?

DODGE: I was a boy once, wasn't I? If he'd had his father around . . .

JANE: . . . his father wouldn't have

done that to him! I'm glad you've admitted it!

DODGE: I'm not admitting anything!

JANE: Too late!

DODGE: If anyone's done him harm, it's you!

JANE: Really?

DODGE: . . . stopping him coming to his own birthday party! How's he supposed to understand what's going on in your sick mind? Don't try and make him feel guilty. He's a happy kid. What are you trying to do to him?

JANE: If he'd been playing around with someone his own age, I wouldn't give a toss . . .

DODGE: Oh? What's the difference?

JANE: You're a bloody grown up, aren't you! You should leave kids alone, shouldn't you?

DODGE: I'm not into kids. You should know that, for Christ's sake! You've got a bloody short memory, you know that? Look! Simon started it . . .

JANE: For God's sake!

DODGE: . . . he wanted it! I just didn't say no! It was all over in seconds. You know how fast I come sometimes. There's no point in making a song and dance about it years after the event!

JANE: Years?

DODGE: When do you think this all happened?

JANE: Jesus! How many others have there been?

DODGE: What others?

JANE: Other children.

DODGE: None! Of course there haven't.There aren't going to be any either.

JANE: How do you know?

DODGE: Because I know! It was a one-off. Anyway, you can't talk about what's good and what isn't.

JANE: Why?

DODGE: All those books you let him read. And the videos.

JANE: What books?

DODGE: The first time we went off into the country, the poor kid was struggling along with a great, fat book about the Manson murders!

JANE: *Helter Skelter*?

DODGE: Yes. Great stuff for a kid. Rape, mass murder, torture . . .

JANE: He can read what he likes.

DODGE: Yes! I know! And the videos. Good way of shutting him up, is it? Drugs, orgies and mutilation? I suppose you call that educational?

JANE: I don't know what he gets from the video shop.

DODGE: Well, you ought to! You're his mother!

JANE: I never tried to stop him watching what he wanted. Books, films . . . it's up to him.

DODGE: Exactly! And all he's done is go from what he's seen on your television into real life. Lucky it was only sex he was interested in! He might have wanted to cut me up! You know what you taught him? Sex is cruel, without feeling, something you take when you need it! Even violently!

JANE: Load of shit!

DODGE: I've taught him about love, affection, caring for someone. You don't like that, do you? I remember what it was like together. Me giving, you taking. Grasp, grasp, grasp! Your husband walked out. I'm getting out too. As far away from you as possible.

JANE: Pedalling away on your bike. A little child with his special toy!

DODGE: The most perfect machine!

JANE: I've been reporting cases of child abuse, and God knows, child murder . . .

DODGE: For fuck's sake!

JANE: . . . it makes me sick! And angry! And now it's happened to my own son! I'd like to strike you dead!

There is a mechanical click from the tape recorder.

DODGE: What was that?

JANE: What?

DODGE *goes over to* JANE*'s bag*

and searches it. He finds the tape recorder.

DODGE: Christ!

JANE: Give me that!

DODGE *takes out the tape cassette.*

DODGE: You filthy fucking bitch!

She tries to grab it from him but he smashes it open and the tape unspools as he tries to rip it to bits.
JANE goes for the knife on the table but is stopped by DODGE who throws her to the floor.
He continues ripping the tape.

DODGE: Fuck you! Fuck you! Why don't you leave me in peace?

JANE: I'll never forgive you!

DODGE (*holding up the tape*): I suppose you get used to playing this sort of trick in your business? All part of a day's work? What were you going to do with it?

JANE: Take it to the police!

DODGE: Bugger off out of here!

JANE (*recovering her tape recorder and her shoulder bag*): If you've turned him queer . . .

DODGE: He's mad on girls! Ask him about Brook Shields!

JANE: Who?

DODGE: Things don't happen like that!

JANE: How do you know? How can you be sure? I may have made mistakes, but, by God, I'll protect him from you! I don't want to hear from you ever again. If you attempt to contact Simon, I'll go straight to the police. Do you understand?

JANE storms out, leaving the door open.
DODGE, in a state of shock, starts to gather up the bits of tape cassette and the torn recording tape. He is unsure how to dispose of the evidence. As he is hiding the bits in one of the boxes, the outer door bell rings. He turns and a child's yellow and blue BMX wheel rolls through the door and lands at his feet.
RIKKI enters.

RIKKI: It's me! Can I make a phone call?

DODGE *beckons him in to do what he wants. RIKKI goes to the phone and dials his agency.*

Hello? Rikki. Hammersmith still. No, I've finished for the night. You never warned me that cunt was into water sports! (*Aside to* DODGE) He wanted to piss on me!
You did know! He told me the other guy you sent played. I don't know. Jimmy, or Alex, maybe? I thumped him. Twice. Once in the belly and once with my knee on the way down. He got heavy with me! I was being reasonable! I'm not doing nothing I don't want to do. He wasn't pleased. He said sorry. Yes. I'll come round tomorrow. Pick my money up, right?

RIKKI *replaces the receiver.*

Got all your problems sorted out, then? Feeling sorry for yourself?

RIKKI *approaches* DODGE *cautiously.* DODGE *recoils each time* RIKKI *tries to touch him.* RIKKI *has to coax* DODGE *into trusting him to massage his temples and the sides of his face.*

Easy. Easy now. Come on. It's only me. That's better. Lay your head back. That's it. They like this. Calms most of them down. You know. Rikki says Relax! Blimey! You're shaking. What's she done to you?

DODGE: Nothing.

RIKKI: Do you ever tell the truth?

DODGE: Of course I do.

RIKKI: . . . he lied . . . Seen the last of her?

DODGE: I hope so.

RIKKI: Is that better?

DODGE: Ummm.

RIKKI: What about this bike, then? Like to get my leg over. Try it for size. Where are the wheels, then?

DODGE: Next door.

RIKKI: I'll get them.

RIKKI *goes to look for the wheels next door.*

DODGE: They're behind the boxes.

RIKKI (*off*): Where?

DODGE: By the wheel jig.

RIKKI: Got them!

RIKKI comes back with a front and back wheel, each beautifully made.

These are wicked! You make them?

DODGE: Yes.

DODGE fetches out the bicycle frame, which is set on its own free-standing jig. RIKKI passes him the back wheel. DODGE slips it on, using quick release hubs. RIKKI passes him the front wheel and DODGE puts that on. He fetches a frame pump from one of the work benches and passes it to RIKKI.

DODGE: Give the back one plenty of air.

RIKKI pumps the rear tyre busily.

RIKKI: You'll never guess what I've got on underneath this lot! Is that enough?

DODGE: Yes.

RIKKI replaces the valve cap and passes the pump to DODGE. While DODGE is putting the pump back, RIKKI slips out of his clothes to reveal the one-piece racing suit that he has on underneath. He shows himself off to DODGE.

RIKKI: Well! Is it me?

DODGE releases the bike from the jig. RIKKI picks it up off the jig and holds it up above his head and turns round a couple of times.

RIKKI: Blimey! It's as light as a feather!

He sets the bike down and DODGE, standing at the front of the bike, with the front wheel between his knees and the handlebars firmly in his hands, beckons RIKKI to get on. RIKKI mounts the bike nimbly while DODGE holds it upright.

DODGE: How does that feel?

RIKKI: Fantastic!

DODGE: Imagine the sun shining on your back. There's no traffic. Mile after mile is passing by and you're feeling strong and full of energy. Some trees are overhanging the road. Watch out for a load of insects! You have to squint to stop them getting in your eyes. As soon as you're out in the sunlight again, they're gone.

RIKKI: Good!

DODGE: Then you pass some banks covered in meadowsweet. There's a lovely smell. Enough to make you drunk!

RIKKI sniffs deeply.

There's a farm ahead! The road is covered in mud and cow dung. You have to slow down a bit. Try to find a clean path through it all. Farm yard smells!

RIKKI: Poo!

DODGE: There's a wood fire burning in the house. Wood smoke! Then you're past and away. And you start to fly down a long, straight hill!

RIKKI: Weee!

*DODGE leans forward and kisses the top of RIKKI's head.
RIKKI leaps off the seat and throws his arms around DODGE and hugs him.*

RIKKI: How much is it worth?

DODGE: £350 to you. A bargain.

RIKKI: Bloody hell!

RIKKI stops hugging DODGE and wheels the bicycle away.

I think I'll stick to nicking them!

RIKKI rests the bicycle up against the table and admires it.

DODGE: Do you want to ride it?

RIKKI: Yes! Can we go off for the day sometime?

DODGE: Where would you like to go?

RIKKI: Southend?

DODGE: Too much traffic. Bikes get nicked when you get there. I'd rather go by train.

RIKKI: Where then?

DODGE: Let's go west. I've got some great routes. Off the main roads, mostly.

RIKKI: OK.

DODGE: Are you serious?

RIKKI: Yes.

DODGE: You wouldn't last thirty miles.

RIKKI: I would! Let's go tomorrow and I'll prove it!

DODGE: Tell you what! Tomorrow we'll go off on a shorter run. Twenty miles or so. Check out the bikes.

RIKKI: OK.

DODGE: See how that goes.

RIKKI: Got to fetch my money in the morning. They owe us quite a bit. Let's go in the afternoon.

DODGE: Come here for two o'clock.

RIKKI: Right! Had a job finding out how to get into this! (*Meaning the one-piece racing suit.*) Drove the other guy wild! He said I'd have to shave my legs. Why do they do that? Does it make you go faster?

DODGE: Lessening the wind resistance?

RIKKI: Wouldn't make that much difference, would it?

DODGE: If you fall off and have to have bandages stuck all over, you can pull them off again without pulling your hairs out.

RIKKI: Is that it?

DODGE: Vanity too.

RIKKI: Do you shave yours? Let's have a look.

RIKKI *lifts up* DODGE's *tracksuit bottoms to have a look.*

DODGE: Used to. Haven't bothered lately.

RIKKI: You haven't had your massage yet.

DODGE: Oh God! Do I have to?

RIKKI: 'course you do! Take your clothes off!

RIKKI *fetches his bag and starts to lay out his things for business. He produces a large towel, which he flaps before laying it out on the floor. A small cloud of talc flies into the air. He sets a cushion at one end of the towel. He gets out various talcs, oils, intensive-care creams, deodorants and finally a soft toilet roll.* DODGE *has been watching this performance without undressing.*

RIKKI: Come on!

RIKKI *goes over and takes him by the hand and drags him to his feet.*

DODGE *takes off his tracksuit and top. He is left wearing his Y-Fronts.*

DODGE: Which way up?

RIKKI: On your belly.

DODGE *tries to make himself comfortable on the floor with the cushion.* RIKKI *puts talc on his hands and rubs it in. He then takes a spray-on deodorant and sprays it on* DODGE's *feet and under his armpits.* RIKKI *then takes the talc and sprinkles it all over* DODGE's *back. He kneels down and starts the massage. After a while,* DODGE *speaks.*

DODGE: You think you're going to get a new bike out of this!

RIKKI: Shut your face!

DODGE: Well you're not!

RIKKI *carries on with his work.*

RIKKI: I've always wanted an older man in my life, Tony. You know. Some one to look up to, show me things. Take me out. Not all the time. Just occasionally. You know? I don't want someone gay. Never leave you alone. Well . . . probably not gay . . . wouldn't mind . . . as long as it was safe. Personally, I'm a safe sex stud. That's what I call myself. You listening?

DODGE: Ummm . . .

RIKKI: Tony . . .

DODGE: Umm?

RIKKI: You know I was telling you about my father.

DODGE: Umm.

RIKKI: There's other things too. I had my own room, you know. For the first time. I'd always slept in a dormitory with the other boys at the Home. It took some getting used to. Being on my own and that. I'd been with my new parents for about a year. Really settled in. Then, one night, my dad came into my bedroom and started chatting and that. And then he kind of slipped his hand into my pyjamas and started playing with my cock. I was dead embarrassed. I just kind of froze. I wasn't exactly innocent. Not after all those years in the Home. But I wasn't expecting that from my dad. He used to do all sorts to me. He went down on me. He never tried to get inside, thank God. I think my mum guessed, but I never said anything. She was scared of him. Sometimes he'd have a drinking party with his mates. One of them used to come up to my room. I think dad must have told him. And he used to put fifty pence by my bedside and then go down on me. I used to let him. God knows what he got out of it. My cock must have stuck up like . . . like . . .

DODGE: A small white thumb.

RIKKI: Small white thumb? I suppose it did. How did you know that, then? From your Simon? Christ!

RIKKI: You're not into kids, are you?

DODGE: Don't you start.

RIKKI: You're not, are you?

DODGE: No.

RIKKI: Honest?

DODGE: Honest.

RIKKI: That's good. Chaos here.

RIKKI *starts playing with some of the unopened letters.*

I've always loved getting letters. No one every used to write to me at the Home. When my birthday came round I used to hope that something would come in the post. It never did. Got cards from the other kids. We did that for each other. Not the same as the postman bringing you something. From outside. I used to think they knew where I was. My real parents. Like they were testing me. To see if I really loved them. I thought they'd come one day and take me away. Maybe they'd write to me. Tell me they hadn't forgotten me.

RIKKI *starts to open a brown envelope.*

Bike mag . . .
You know I said I wanted to get married and that?

DODGE: You haven't finished the massage.

RIKKI: . . . have kids and that . . . Well, you know in films and on the tele and that . . . stories . . . you know . . . kids kind of fall in love with one another, don't they. I know it sounds daft. Well

. . . it doesn't happen. Not to me. Never been in love with anyone. Not like you're supposed to. Just sex. Bodies. Coming off. Together. Alone. It's dead. If it was ever in me. I don't love anyone. I don't know how. I'm different. They done it to me. That's what I think.

I was so abused, Mr Dodge!

RIKKI *opens another large envelope. Inside he finds a collection of photographs of little boys.*

RIKKI: What's this, then?

DODGE: Christ!

RIKKI: Who are all these little kids?

DODGE: I don't know. Give me that.

RIKKI: What do you do with these then?

DODGE: I didn't know they were there.

RIKKI: You said you wasn't into kids. You fucking liar!

DODGE: I don't know where they came from.

RIKKI *throws the photos at* DODGE, *who tries to pick them up.* RIKKI *goes over to the piles of boxes in a fury.*

RIKKI: What else have you got hidden away?

DODGE: Nothing. Look! Leave my stuff alone!

RIKKI *finds a box with more photos and magazines of naked boys. He picks one up and waves it in* DODGE*'s face.*

RIKKI: Fucking hell! Look at this! Look at this!

RIKKI *empties the box over* DODGE*'s head.*

You said Simon was a one-off! You fucking liar!

DODGE *slaps* RIKKI*'s face.*

RIKKI: Don't you fucking hit me!

RIKKI *hurls himself at* DODGE, *who parries a couple of punches before throwing* RIKKI *across the room.*

RIKKI: I trusted you! I wanted you to be my mate!

RIKKI *is very distressed and gets dressed as quickly as he can.*

RIKKI: I thought you was going to be good to me. Going off on the bikes and that. You're just another fucking pevert! Bent bastard! Little boys with little cocks. Only good for peeing! Off your fucking head good and proper. Just a fucking witch, you are! Stick them in the oven, do you? Turn them into ginger bread? Little kids who've lost their way?

DODGE: Take the bike! Take it!

RIKKI: Fuck the bike!

DODGE: You can have it. I'm sorry.

RIKKI: You tricked me. That's it! Finished!

DODGE: It's not like you think.

RIKKI: Shit!

DODGE: Why don't you listen?

RIKKI: You think you can talk yourself out of any bloody corner. I know, see? I know what happens!

DODGE: I'm sorry about what happened to you. That wasn't me.

RIKKI: Whose kids are these, then? What do you do? Wank over them?

DODGE: I don't know.

RIKKI: 'course you do! There's no one in the world you can trust! Just men after your body!

DODGE: I can help you, Rikki.

RIKKI: Like shit!

DODGE: Take the bike. Try it out.

RIKKI: I wanted some one to talk to. Some one to listen.

DODGE *gathers up* RIKKI'*s things and stuffs them in his bag.*

DODGE: Please go now.

DODGE *tosses* RIKKI *his bag.* RIKKI *picks it up and reaches into a side pocket.*

RIKKI: You need cutting up! You know that?

DODGE: Fuck off!

RIKKI *suddenly pulls the knife out of the side pocket of the bag and holds it at* DODGE'*s throat. He forces* DODGE *onto the floor.*

RIKKI: Look at you! You daft shit! Fuck little kids, would you? What with? What with, Mr Dodge? Some one ought to cut it off and stuff it down your throat! Is that what you'd like? Like a bit of blood, do you?

DODGE *is terrified on the floor.* RIKKI *leaves him and goes over to the wallet and takes all the money.*

What have you done, then? Followed kids around the park? Watched them coming out of school? Pocket full of sweets, Mr Dodge? Get dressed, you look horrible!

DODGE *goes towards* RIKKI *who is going through the wallet.* RIKKI *sticks his knife out.*

Yea? Yea? Back off!

DODGE: It's not like that. You've got it wrong. I don't do anything like that.

RIKKI: Oh yes?

DODGE: I'm not a danger to anyone.

RIKKI *has found a photo of Simon in the wallet. He holds it out. When* DODGE *comes close to take it,* RIKKI *throws it at him scornfully.* DODGE *picks it up.*

DODGE: Who says it's not natural, Simon and me? He's entitled to his own body, his emotions, his feelings. You ought to know that, for Christ's sake! If Simon wants me . . . It's important to him! I am! I'm part of his life! There are plenty of kids like Simon who need a mate. That's what I was. We were good for one another and balls to anyone who says we weren't! It may be finished . I think it probably is finished. But we didn't get our sums wrong!

RIKKI: Bollocks!

DODGE: Whatever they say. Whatever you think! You think you're very smart. Know everything, don't you! Well you ought to know something after what's happened to you! All you do is go crazy! Waving that fucking knife around! Scaring the shit out of me!

RIKKI: Good!

DODGE: You've met me ten years too late! Mr UB40! Judo champ! Mr Magic Fingers! I cared for him. I loved him.

He wasn't getting it from her. From anyone else . . .

RIKKI: Ten years too late?

DODGE: I'd have done you good.

RIKKI: Done me good and proper! Climbing up the stairs with fifty pence in your hand.

DODGE: Not like that. Don't blame me for what they did. That wasn't me.

RIKKI: Never is you!

DODGE: I'd have given you what you were looking for.

RIKKI: What was that?

DODGE: Taken you out on trips. Cared for you. Fed you. Cleaned you up.

RIKKI: My mum done that for me.

DODGE: I'd have treated you well. Honest. I would.

RIKKI: I know why! You'd have got at me. Little by little. Being nice and that. Getting me where you wanted. Cleaned me up, would you? In and out of the bathroom? No thanks. I could do that for myself, Mr Dodge.

DODGE: Sure. Of course you could.

RIKKI: And all the time you'd be waiting for your chance to get in! Hopping around like a spider! A treat. A trip. A present. Ever so nice! At least those guys with their money didn't promise one thing and take another. They did come to the point, Mr Dodge. More honest than you'll ever be. It was simple. Just trade. No emotions. No feelings. Me selling. Them buying. Just part of life, wasn't it? Like what grown-ups was doing in shops and that. Business. A good start, having some money in your pocket.

DODGE: Exactly what I'm getting away from.

RIKKI: This crazy trip of yours. What are you going to do when it's finished? Go round again in the other direction?

RIKKI *whirls his hand round in an anti-clockwise direction.*

This way?

DODGE: I don't know.

RIKKI: You were lucky. Just now you were. Something inside me wanted to cut you up!

DODGE: Why didn't you?

RIKKI: I'm not really into murder. If I was, you'd be done by now good and proper. Close thing. You want to be careful, Mr Dodge. You could get yourself into trouble!

DODGE: I'm ashamed of all this (*meaning the child pornography*). I am. I wanted to find out what was going on inside me. I didn't know how to get rid of it. Couldn't put it in the bin. Someone might find it. Thought about burning it. Someone might see. I was going to put it in someone else's bin. Thought someone might catch me. I used to wish Jane and me would get back together again. Not any more! Maybe someone else will turn up. I'm not interested in men, Rikki. I wish I was sometimes. Might make things easier. I've played with the idea. Escort agencies. The odd masseur. Just playing games. Doesn't work for me. Then Simon comes back into my life, bouncing into the shop, excited, full of his chatter. He throws himself at me. Jumps on my lap with his comics. I have to read to him. *Bash Street Kids*. *Wizzer and Chips*. *Spiderman*. He's really made me love him. He worked at it night and day. He picked me out, Rikki. I never went after him. He chose me. He honoured me. I couldn't refuse him, Rikki. Why do people hate me for loving him? What do they know? Now I've lost almost everything. They'd wipe me out if they could. I'm surprised at you, though. I didn't expect that from you.

RIKKI: About tomorrow.

DODGE: Yes.

RIKKI: I shouldn't have done what I done. But I'd really like . . .

DODGE: On the bikes?

RIKKI: Can we?

DODGE: If you want.

RIKKI: Yes. I've seen them wizzing past. I watch the bikes on Channel Four, you know. Honest! I do! It won't happen again . . . you know . . .

RIKKI *throws his knife onto* DODGE*'s pile of junk.*

DODGE: Should I phone him again?

RIKKI: Little Simon?

DODGE: Yes.

RIKKI: No. Leave him alone.

DODGE: You reckon?

RIKKI: Don't stir it up. Let it settle,
Tony. He'll find his own bunch of
mates. He won't cause no trouble.
Probably sting you for a few quid when
he's short.

DODGE: You know about these things?

RIKKI: Had to, didn't I! Tell you what.
Let's meet up around 11.30 tomorrow
morning. Can't make it any earlier.
Got to get my money. I'll come round
here, right?

DODGE: OK.

RIKKI: Tony, you couldn't stick on a pair
of toe clips, could you?

DODGE: Yes.

RIKKI *gets the money he's stolen
out of his back pocket and throws it on
the table.*

DODGE: Thanks.

RIKKI *picks up his bag and prepares
to leave.*

RIKKI: Right! Mr Dodge! Tony. Sir.

DEKKA AND DAVA

Characters

DEKKA, *aged 13*
DAVA, *aged 12*
INSPECTOR MURK
HASSEL ⎫   *Members of*
CLAP ⎬   *'Tinned Rat'*
FLOP   ⎭   *Theatre Company*
OLD LADY
MAM

Author's Note

I gave up teaching at a school in West Newcastle at the beginning of May 1974. I had decided to become a playwright, but at that time hadn't written a single play. Nor was I sure exactly how to write one.

I went into Newcastle Central Library each day and wrote *Dekka and Dava* in biro in an exercise book. I showed the script to playwright C.P. Taylor, who was then literary advisor to the Tyneside Theatre Company. He liked it and as a result I was offered a commission to write a play for performance around schools in the region. That was how my professional career started.

Looking back at the play 13 years later, I am appalled (and privately amused) by the crude political posturing and surprised at the level of fantasy, not since repeated. The broad dialect of my pupils at school is still loud and clear in my head. The way the two boys play off against each other is a dry run for Phil and Robert in *Rents* (written a year later) and Donald and Andy in *Accounts* (two years later). Not surprisingly, *Dekka and Dava* has never been performed professionally.

Michael Wilcox, 1987

The sound of a cat purring. INSPECTOR MURK *enters. The cat is at once silent.*

MURK: Puss puss ... puss puss puss. Where are you? Come on. I know you're here. Playing little games with me? I'll find you.

He darts across the room and looks under the desk. It's still silent.

Thought I had you then.

The cat mews from the other side of the room.

Oh ...

MURK *walks slowly over to where the noise is coming from. When he gets close, the cat screams and hisses in a violent manner.* MURK *takes a couple of steps back in alarm.*

Damn you ... I need you today. There's work to be done ...

The cat starts purring with pleasure at the thought of work.

I knew that would please you. Be careful, black cat. I am more dangerous than you. Come when I call. Don't play games with Inspector Murk ... no one mucks around with Murk. Cross my path and it'll be unlucky for you. Silence ...

The cat stops purring.

... and see who I've got for you today.

MURK *sits at his desk and presses the switch on his intercom.*

VOICE: Yes, sir?

MURK: Send them in ...

VOICE: Yes, Sir.

Two scruffy boys enter. They stand defiantly in front of MURK.

MURK: Look at the state of that ... my God. Well ... you've done it this time. Oh dear me. You have. Rotten little bastards! There's blood on your shirts. Look ... look! You're impregnated. BLOOD!

MURK *flips through their files.*

Not a pretty story. Truancy ... thieving. So ... your speciality is stealing cars, is it Derek?

DEKKA: Dekka.

MURK: What?

DEKKA: My name's Dekka, not Derek.

MURK: I'll call you what I like, sonny Jim. Don't you give me any of your lip either.

DEKKA: What difference does it make now?

MURK: SIR!

DEKKA: Dekka, not sir ...

MURK: You call me SIR, you degenerate bastard.

DAVA: He's no bastard ... he's my brother.

MURK: So you've got a tongue as well, have you David?

DAVA: Dava ...

MURK (*hissing like a cat*): Bastard ... bastard ... David.

DAVA: Dava.

MURK: SIR ...

DAVA: Dava.

MURK: Murder ... murder. We're going to throw the book at you this time. You'll pay for every drop of blood you've shed. We're going to move in on you. We're going to find out everything about you. Where you've been. Who you've spoken to. Where you've been sleeping. I'll unearth little crimes you've scarcely thought of. Half considered crimes. Crimes that lurk in the shadows of your black minds, which darken your souls. I'll prise them out and we'll catalogue them until your entire persons are captured in our files. Then, with your statements still wet and the details racing into our computers, we'll punish you for your sins. Harshly. Without mercy. You will be anatomised. Neutered. We're full of little tricks. Have you sold your bodies? We'll see. We have doctors. You will be examined, you little buggers, to see what can be found ...

DEKKA: Shit ...

DAVA: ... most likely.

MURK: We can find more than that.

The cat screams.

DEKKA *and* DAVA's *house in*
Newcastle upon Tyne. It's about 4.30.
MAM's *out at her afternoon job at the*
launderama and DA *doesn't get in until*
7. The boys rush in.

DEKKA: Beat you.

DAVA: Did not.

DEKKA: Did an'all.

DAVA: It was me that spotted big Betty
hangin' oot hor washing.

DEKKA: Massive boobs on that woman.

DAVA: Why hasn't wor Ma got massive
tits?

DEKKA: Divven be cheeky aboot wor
Ma, ye cheeky git. Anyway, it's alus
other people's Ma's got big tits, nivver
ye own. 'Tisn't natural.

DAVA: It's natural on Billy's Ma.

DEKKA: Billy's a freak.

DAVA: Watch it. He's me mate.

DEKKA: Aye. He's a freak.

DAVA: Cheeky nawt.

DEKKA: Ah piss ov.

DAVA: Pissov yersel.

DEKKA: Play you at brag.

DAVA: Three carder.

DEKKA: Aye.

DAVA: Whose cards?

DEKKA: Mine.

DAVA: MINE!

DEKKA: Alreet. Please yersel. Fog deal.

DAVA: My fog deal . . . they're wor
cards.

DEKKA: Alreet.

DAVA: There yer are.

DEKKA: What a load of shite.

DAVA: I've got a great hand, me.

DEKKA: You dealt them, you little cheat.

DAVA: Ah nivver cheat, me.

DEKKA: You slipped that King.

DAVA: Did I shite.

DEKKA: Did an'all. Ah saw yer!

DAVA: Nivver in the world.

DEKKA: Ah've had enough . . . Ah'm
sick.

DAVA: Ah'm hungry.

DEKKA: Fancy some scran?

DAVA: Aye . . . what you got?

DEKKA: Nawt mysel.

DAVA: As usual. Yer wouldn't even give
a dyin' old man a fruit gum.

DEKKA: Divven fancy fruit gums, do I.

DAVA: Fancied mine the other neet.

DEKKA: Won'em at brag. Gave 'em to
me tart after.

DAVA: Yer tart! Who's yer tart noo, like?

DEKKA: Linda MaCree.

DAVA: Linda MaCree! That old bag?
Gawd . . . what a witch. I couldn't shag
hor if she was the last tart on earth.

DEKKA: Yer wouldn't know how ter shag
hor if yer tried, yer little poof.

DAVA: Ah . . . nic off.

DEKKA: Wor Ma's got some scran. Let's
take a look.

DAVA: Aye. Thieving noo. Yer know
your trouble? You're a delinquent. I'll
get the welfare onto you.

DEKKA: Least they'll not catch us like
the wag man nabbed ye last Friday.
You didn't half look daft getting out of
the police van outside the school.

DAVA: That was Billy's fault, that.
He said the launderama was safe on a
rainy day.

DEKKA: Daft git! Yer know wor Ma
sweeps the place out of an afternoon.
Every Ma on the estate goes there for
a bit chat an' that. Bound to get caught.

DAVA: It was wet.

DEKKA: Look at this.

DAVA: Steak . . .

DEKKA: . . . for wor Da.

DAVA: Only one.

DEKKA: What aboot us then?

DAVA: We're not gettin' any.

DEKKA: As usual.

DAVA: Beans wi' Ma . . .

DEKKA: . . . an' a cup of tea . . .

DAVA: ... chips wi' the lads at 9 ...

DEKKA: ... football behind the garages ...

DAVA: Ball's burst.

DEKKA: Ne football then.

DAVA: Ah'm starving.

DEKKA: Ah could stuff that steak ...

DAVA: ... up yer bum.

DEKKA: When did we last have steak?

DAVA: Ah divven na ...

DEKKA: ... nivver ...

DAVA: ... in living memory.

DEKKA: She'll be back ...

DAVA: ... in half an hour ...

DEKKA: ... at the earliest.

DAVA: Wor Da'll kill us.

DEKKA: He will anyway if he's as pissed as he was last neet.

DAVA: Maybe he'll be palatic again and not want ne scran ...

DEKKA: Howay.

DAVA: Howay the lads!

DEKKA: How do you cook the bugger?

DAVA: Here ... let me do it.

DEKKA: Howay. Hands off.

DAVA: Kick yer heed in in a minute.

DEKKA: Stick it in the oven.

DAVA: Grill it, yer daft git.

DEKKA: Oh aye, grilled steak.

DAVA: Put some salt on.

DEKKA: Not too much.

DAVA: And some pepper.

DEKKA: Divven like pepper.

DAVA: Ah love it, me.

DEKKA: Well ah divvent.

DAVA: Alreet, we'll compromise.

DEKKA: What's compromise?

DAVA: I'll put pepper on one side but not the other ... there.

DEKKA: Grill's scorching hot.

DAVA: Proper little Fanny Cradock ye!

DEKKA: Fanny yersel ...

DAVA: Stick it under there.

DEKKA: Ah'll di it from now on.

DAVA: Hark at it sizzle.

DEKKA: By ... have a niff of that.

DAVA: Let's eat it now. Ah cannot wait.

DEKKA: Piss ov. Turn it over ...

DAVA: Look at all the blood.

DEKKA: You're corrupt. You're all food and violence.

DAVA: It's burnin' man, whatye doin'?

DEKKA: Fetch us a plate. Quick.

DAVA: Ah cannot find one ...

DEKKA: Hurry Dava man.

DAVA: There yer are. Divvent tell us ... you bornt it.

DEKKA: Have not.

DAVA: Give us a sniff.

DEKKA: Hold out the plate.

DEKKA *puts the steak on the plate.*

DAVA: Ahhhhhhh ...

DAVA *drops the plate and the steak. The plate smashes.*

DAVA: ... you bornt us.

DEKKA: Stupid bugger.

DAVA: It was yee!

DEKKA *picks up the steak and tears it roughly in half.*

DEKKA: That's your half.

They both eat the steak ravenously. It's all gone in a moment.

DAVA: That was ...

DEKKA: ... delicious ...

DAVA: ... cushty bloody steak ...

DEKKA: ... divine ...

MAM *comes in through the front door.*

DEKKA: Christ ... the plate ...

DAVA: Mam'll kill us.

DEKKA: Kill ye! You did it.

DAVA: It was you ...

DEKKA: Was not ...

MAM *enters.*

MAM: What's that smell then?

DAVA: What smell?

DEKKA: Ah cannot smell anything.

MAM: Who's smashed that plate?

DAVA: What plate?

DEKKA: Ohhhh . . . you mean that plate?

DAVA: That was him.

DEKKA: You lying git.

DAVA: Christ . . . the stove's still warm.

DEKKA: Aye . . . it's a canny cold evening.

DAVA: Aye, it is Ma.

MAM: You little buggers. So it's come to eating your Da's tea now, has it? Not content with thieving from Tescos like respectable children, you'll thieve from your own father. And I've been working my fingers to the bone to feed youse lot, sweeping out the launderama. Christ . . . what have we done to deserve this?

DEKKA: We get hungry too, yer na.

MAM: Shurrup. When your father comes yem the neet you'll get such a hiding as you've nivver had before. And not content with eating his tea, you've smashed my plate. Now get out of here, you stupid buggers, get the hell out of here. Piss off! Scram!

The boys run out.

Later that night. A derelict house in Elswick. The sound of a flute. Enter HASSEL, CLAP and FLOP into the back yard. FLOP is playing the flute.

HASSEL: Where's this then?

CLAP: Elswick. The whole street is due for demolition.

HASSEL: Give it a rest, Flop.

FLOP: Sorry.

CLAP: What a place . . . my God.

HASSEL: Did you cut your mouth, Clap?

FLOP: When you chewed up that glass?

CLAP: No.

HASSEL: The people were really repelled by that . . . a great success in fact.

FLOP: What made you do it?

CLAP: I just felt that a repulsive gesture was needed at that moment in our performance. Anyway, it was plastic, not glass.

HASSEL: That's cheating.

CLAP: They didn't know that. You remember when we were down in Eastbourne and we were entertaining the old people . . .

HASSEL: . . . and Flop picked up their cat . . .

CLAP: . . . and bit it . . .

A cat screams.

FLOP: The cat was real.

HASSEL: That created exactly the sort of resentment that we're after.

CLAP: Biting cats is great when you can get hold of one at the right moment . . .

HASSEL: . . . right . . .

CLAP: . . . but our most significant gesture against the autocratic state . . .

FLOP: . . . and officialdom . . .

CLAP: . . . was in Bath, when we all spontaneously pissed on the double yellow lines in the High Street.

FLOP: Wouldn't it have been more effective if it hadn't been 2 o'clock in the morning and somebody had seen us?

HASSEL: Oh shut up, Flop.

FLOP: Sorry, Hassel.

HASSEL: The important thing is that we did it. That's what group identity is all about, spontaneous unity of involvement.

FLOP: We'd been boozing for hours.

CLAP: Stop squabbling. The Newcastle Festival starts tomorrow and we'll be working our balls off all day.

HASSEL: Let's just remember who we are. Flop . . .

FLOP plays a few weird notes on his flute.

HASSEL: Tinned Rat.

FLOP and CLAP: Tinned Rat.

CLAP: Tinned rat is safe. It's sterilised, palatable, inoffensive.

HASSEL: An escaped rat . . .

FLOP: . . . a rebel rat . . .

CLAP: . . . a cornered rat . . .

TOGETHER: . . . is dangerous!

FLOP plays a few more notes on his flute. DEKKA and DAVA worm their way under the fencing into the back yard. The group are sitting in meditation apparently not noticing the boys, while FLOP continues with his playing.

DEKKA: Are you a bunch of loonies?

The group continue to meditate. FLOP finishes his playing.

DAVA: Weirdos if you ask me.

DEKKA: Who are they?

DAVA: Divven na . . .

DEKKA: Shall we hop it?

DAVA: If you want.

DEKKA: Maybe they'll let us stay for the night.

DAVA: Well, we're not gannin'yem.

DEKKA: Not too cald the neet.

DAVA: Easy sleep out.

DEKKA: Like them?

DAVA: Ah reckon.

DEKKA: Wonder if they're on the run.

DAVA: Ask 'em.

DEKKA: Ask 'em yersel.

The group break their meditation.

HASSEL: Hello.

DEKKA: You on the run?

HASSEL: Aye.

DAVA: What yer done?

CLAP: Tried to survive.

DAVA: What . . . knocking things an' that?

CLAP: Very occasionally.

FLOP: Who are you?

DEKKA: I'm Dekka.

DAVA: I'm Dava.

HASSEL: Hassel.

CLAP: Clap.

FLOP: Flop.

DEKKA: You sleeping here tonight?

CLAP: Yes.

FLOP: Where are you from?

DEKKA: New Biggin Hall.

DAVA: It's that way.

DEKKA: It's not man, it's over there.

DAVA: Is it shite.

DEKKA: We're on the run . . .

DAVA: . . . from wor Da . . .

DAVA: . . . we ate his tea.

DAVA: Can we stay here the neet?

HASSEL: If you want.

CLAP: Let's light the lanterns and have something to eat.

FLOP: See what I've got in here.

CLAP lights a couple of lanterns while FLOP produces half a dozen bottles of brown ale from his haversack. HASSEL gets out the sandwiches.

DEKKA: Look at all that broon ale!

FLOP: There's one for each of you.

DAVA: Ah divven believe it. Pinch us. It's not true.

DEKKA pinches his bum.

DAVA: Not me bum, ye gom.

HASSEL: Have a sandwich.

DEKKA: What are they?

HASSEL: Pâté and cucumber.

DEKKA: Divven like foreign food.

DAVA: We'll just stick to the booze.

DEKKA: Aye.

HASSEL: Are the police out looking for you?

DAVA: No chance.

DEKKA: Wor Da'll nivver bring them in.

DAVA: He might take the morrow off work to look for us.

DEKKA: Not because he cares, like . . .

DAVA: . . . but if we're missing too long, he'll get into trouble with the welfare.

DEKKA: Kids on wor estate are often away . . .

DAVA: . . . aye . . .

DEKKA: . . . something just snaps an' they're off.

DAVA: It's school, the teccers, the police . . . it's all grown ups.

DEKKA: They don't want to know.

DAVA: They're onto you the whole time.

CLAP: What's wrong with the teachers?

DAVA: Boring and bossy.

DEKKA: Just divven like them.

DAVA: Most of them.

DEKKA: The best move on.

DAVA: It's alus the worst that stay longest.

DEKKA: They want us to think their thoughts.

DAVA: We want to think our own.

DEKKA: Who are you lot then?

FLOP: We tour the country with songs, music, demonstrations . . .

CLAP: We aim to amuse, provoke and repulse our audiences.

DEKKA: Do you get paid?

HASSEL: We get a grant from the Arts Council.

DAVA: Wor Da works for the council an'all.

DEKKA: Good money is it?

DAVA: Cannot be if they live like this.

FLOP: We don't always live like this.

CLAP: Sleeping rough is our contribution to the Newcastle Festival.

DAVA: Who writes your jokes an' that?

DEKKA: Who's in charge?

HASSEL: We're a democratic group. We decide things among ourselves.

DEKKA: Democratic? That's to do with democracy, isn't it?

DAVVA: Divven talk to us about democracy. We had that at school last Thorsday.

DEKKA: Aye . . . we wer told in assembly that we would have a students' council that would be elected democratically. It would meet and decide things an' that.

DAVA: We elected Billy.

DEKKA: He's a freak, you see.

DAVA: Not half as big a freak as him!

DEKKA: Anyway, the council met and democratically decided to abolish school uniform . . .

DAVA: . . . but the head teccer overruled them and said that the uniform . . .

DEKKA: . . . which hardly anyone wears anyway . . .

DAVA: . . . should stay.

DEKKA: So don't mention that dorty word democracy to us because we've found out what it really means.

DAVA: Aye . . . if you democratically decide on what the boss wants, it's ok . . .

DEKKA: . . . but if it isn't what he wants you might as well piss off!

HASSEL: Anyone else want the last sandwich? No? I'll eat it then.

DAVA: This beer's making us sleepy.

DEKKA: Yer alus sleepy you.

DAVA: Getting chilly an'all.

FLOP: Let's go into the house and sing some songs.

DEKKA: He sings, don't you.

DAVA: Do I nic.

DEKKA: Get him to sing Danny Boy. You've nivver hord aut like it.

The group gather up their things and start to carry the lanterns into the house. DEKKA and DAVA are the last to go in.

DAVA: Dekka, man, come here. Look up at them stars.

DEKKA: Seen them before.

DAVA: Look up again. There's nothing between us and them but space.

FLOP's flute is heard from the house playing a lament. The boys follow the sound into the house.

Sound of a purring cat. Enter MURK.

MURK: So they spent the night in Elswick, you say, and the next couple of days playing around the town, taking refuge in Marks and Spencers, knocking things from the covered market and sneaking through the side doors of cinemas. Oh, I've heard it all before. Nothing escapes Murk. The shadows of crimes fall across my desk each morning and drift through my dreams at night. But I have all the most efficient forces at my disposal, all the latest technology, everything needed for the purification of the race. But what happened next? I've seen them in Playland by The Golden Fleece trying their luck at the rent game. I have seen them scrounging from chip shops and sleeping on building sites. They spent a couple of nights in the back of a lorry you know . . .

The cat mews.

What's that?

It mews again.

Really? Oh you're right. They are no young innocents. I've no sympathy for them. They are the third and fourth generation of skivers, criminals, wife-beating, kid-bashing boozers. Their father's a leech on the Welfare State. Their grandfather knew the inside of Durham Gaol better than Scotswood. It's all there in our files.

If the present generation of potential vermin keep their noses clean, work moderately hard and think only of horses, football, brown ale and tarts, I'll leave them alone. But if they cross no man's land, they cross me. If they attempt to break out of the council estates, form action committees, start using words instead of fists and bottles, then I know I'll need reinforcements. We've got plenty of heavies who have been conditioned by our training to obey every order. We've got the latest computerised technology that can reduce God himself to a statistic. But heaven help us if we are forced to recruit intellectuals as well! A hundred fists cannot touch one good idea, and there's the real danger. How do you fight an enemy who's scull you cannot crack with one good blow from a truncheon?

So what do we do? We pinch the life of the bud before it blooms. We give the dullest men the top jobs in Education. We recruit the liveliest youngsters into the armed forces and build new council estates so we can concentrate the largest density of the remainder into the smallest possible space. We identify their territory for them so they can be contained,

neutralised, sterilised. So when two new victims present themselves, we must not hesitate to bite and scratch and claw . . .

The cat screams terribly.

The house of an OLD LADY. *The walls are completely covered with photographs of Newcastle, many of which date from the last century. The floor is covered with rag dolls, some of which are very old, which are dressed in the style of young people over many generations. The* OLD LADY *is sitting by the fire and completing her latest doll, which is a replica of* DAVA.

OLD LADY (*singing*): 'Terrible collision on the railway line,
Poor cow didn't see the red light shine,
Oh it happened long ago
And they're working on it now,
Sorting out the engine from the poor old cow.'

I'll give you a nose, my dear, to sniff out the evil of the world.

'Terrible collision on the railway line . . .'

More thread to finish the job. Never leave a job undone. Be thorough.

'Poor cow didn't see the red light shine . . .'

And now some eyes to see in the dark. Eyes that reflect the fire of the soul. Eyes to catch the breath and quicken the heart. Eyes that might have thrilled me long ago.

'Oh it happened long ago
And they're working . . . on it . . . now . . .'

And lastly a mouth to speak the truth the eyes perceive. To tell the tale of lost generations, of energy stifled and misused.

'Sorting out the engine from the . . . poor . . . old . . . cow.'

And there you are finished, my dear. Listen, my children, you have a new brother today. Speak to him kindly. Get to know him well. Try to love him as I have always tried to love you. (*To the doll:*) Don't be frightened, my dear. They'll all be your friends. You will play with them and enjoy the sun in summer and the cold and frost of winter. And I will read you stories that fill the soul with longing and for death. Death! Did you hear me? Look at the walls around you. See the yellowing shadows of those who lived in an old, dead world, haunted by the ghosts of promises made in youth and broken in old age.

And I'm there amongst them. Spot me out if you can. The young girl hiding in the hay field, playing croquet on the lawn, travelling in dog carts to market, standing shyly with gallant, whiskered gentlemen whose pale eyes conceal lecherous hearts.

Church on Sundays. Collects learnt by heart.

I have felt the waspish taunts of the virgin governess whose only delights were the sad fantasies of lonely nights.

You will not grow old.

Don't stare at me, you naughty boy! The moths may get you. Your fabric will fade, men may come who do not know you, to burn you when I am gone. But until then you will always remain young and dream of a future you can never reach.

So what shall we call him? David? Very well. You will be David and will live with me. I shall make you a brother shortly.

There is a clatter from the kitchen.

What's that? Stay here, and not a word, any of you.

She goes to the kitchen door.

You naughty boys! Climbing through my window.

DEKKA (*off*): Quick . . . let's get out!

There is a crash and a yell.

DAVA (*off*): Shit . . . Ah've broke me arm.

OLD LADY: We'll have none of that language here. You must set an example to the children. (*She goes into the kitchen.*) Now come along. Don't argue.

She leads DEKKA and DAVA back into her room. DAVA clutches his arm. They are both very dirty.

DEKKA: Look at the state of that!

OLD LADY: Don't be cheeky! Both of you come and sit by the fire.

DAVA: Oh me arm.

OLD LADY: Show me what you've done. Oh dear . . . dear. Not broken. Only bruised and bleeding a little. I'll clean it up for you.

DAVA: It's alreet, Mrs, just leave it.

DEKKA: Do you live here?

DAVA: Daft question if you ask me.

DEKKA: Didn't did I.

DAVA: Get stuffed.

OLD LADY: That's quite enough of that talk. Dear me, what will the children think?

DEKKA: You got kids then?

OLD LADY: Use your eyes, child.

DEKKA: Them your kids? Them dolls?

OLD LADY: Don't say kids. It's vulgar. They are my children.

DAVA: You've had a lot.

DEKKA: Reckon she's been having it off with a golliwog.

OLD LADY: Disgraceful boy! You should have your mouths washed out with soap and water, both of you. You both need a thorough scrubbing. You're filthy from head to toe.

DAVA: Thought she was a scrubber!

OLD LADY: What have you been up to?

DAVA: That's wor business.

DEKKA: You goin' to call the police, Mrs?

OLD LADY: No. I have other plans for you two.

DEKKA: What like?

DAVA: This place gives me the creeps.

DEKKA: Me too.

DAVA: Reckon she's a witch?

OLD LADY: I'm not saying that you don't both deserve to be severely punished for breaking into my house. I know you were up to no good, so don't try to tell me otherwise.

DAVA: We were hungry.

DEKKA: Give us some scran, Mrs, I'm starving.

OLD LADY: Some what? Ask properly whoever you are.

DEKKA: Dekka.

OLD LADY: You are an odd child. And who are you?

DAVA: Dava.

OLD LADY: David . . . how very strange. I have just made a boy called David. Let me introduce you. David, this boy calls himself Dava.

DAVA: Morning . . .

DEKKA: Daft git, it's afternoon.

DAVA: Afternoon . . . how are you? Alreet son?

DEKKA: Doesn't say very much, does he.

OLD LADY: Don't take any notice of their vulgar speech, David. They'll learn in time. I'll see to that.

DEKKA: Can I say hello an'all, Mrs?

OLD LADY: Of course, my dear.

DEKKA: Hello, David, me ol'son. How's yesel then? Alreet? There's a good kid.

DAVA: Please Mrs, give us some food, Mrs . . . I'm starving.

DEKKA: We only broke in for something to eat.

DAVA: You can hear my belly rumbling half way down the road.

DEKKA: What about mine then? Ah'm just as hungry as ye!

DAVA: Ah divven give a shite about you. If you hadn't been so clumsy down the market, we might have lived off that stuff for weeks.

DEKKA: It was you! You distract, I do the knocking.

DAVA: I was distracting.

DEKKA: Oh aye. He nearly bat ye in the mouth you was so distracting.

DAVA: You were too slow!

DEKKA: Ahhhh piss off!

They start to fight.

OLD LADY: Stop this at once! Animals!

They carry on. The OLD LADY *clouts* DEKKA *across the ear and the boys fall apart angrily. The* OLD LADY *storms into the kitchen.*

DEKKA: It's a mad house this.

DAVA: Is the world full of loonies?

DEKKA: Loonies and soft shites.

DAVA: Which are ye?

DEKKA: Soft shite jus' now.

DAVA: Shall we hop it?

DEKKA: Might as well wait for some scran.

DAVA: She might call the police.

DEKKA: Ne phone, ah divven think.

DEKKA tries the door. It's locked.

DEKKA: The bugger. We're locked in.

DAVA: Nivver!

DEKKA: Prisoners.

DAVA tries the kitchen door. That is locked as well.

DAVA (*shouting*): Hey Mrs . . . You locked us in, ye na!

The OLD LADY *is heard singing away in the kitchen.*

DEKKA: If she tries anything, we've got hor children.

DAVA (*picking up a doll*): Now listen here, ye stuffed git, if your Mrs tries to work horsel with us, I'll pull yer bloody eyes out.

The OLD LADY *enters with two bowls of soup.*

OLD LADY: Soup . . . soup for boys with clean hands.

DEKKA: Not washing mine.

DAVA: Me neither.

OLD LADY: It's delicious. Can't you smell it? It's just what you want.

DEKKA: Smells great.

DAVA: Aye.

OLD LADY: Clean hands. Set an example.

DAVA: Howay . . .

The boys go into the kitchen.

OLD LADY: Did you see them? Did you watch them closely? It's a cruel world outside. That's what will happen to you if you ever leave me!

The boys return.

OLD LADY: Now you may have the soup.

They gulp it down greedily. It's all gone.

DEKKA: Lovely.

DAVA: That was great.

DEKKA: Thanks, Mrs, we'll be going now.

OLD LADY: Go? Go where?

DAVA: Yem.

OLD LADY: You're not going home. You know that. Never try to fool old people. We have more wisdom than you know.

DEKKA: Where we gan is wor business.

DAVA: You cannot keep us here.

DEKKA: You locked us in.

DAVA: Prisoners.

OLD LADY: There is more freedom here than outside in the city.

DEKKA: Locked in a room . . .

DAVA: . . . divven be mad!

OLD LADY: Out there you will be hunted . . . tracked . . . sniffed out. They will get you, run as you may. Here you will be warm, have plenty of food and friends, and I will love you.

DEKKA: Shag an old bag like hor!

DAVA: Get in!

DEKKA: Thanks all the same, Mrs . . . We must be gannin' now.

DAVA: Aye.

DEKKA: That door's locked, remember.

DAVA: Let's get out through the kitchen window.

DEKKA: Mad house this.

OLD LADY: Stay where you are!

She prevents them from leaving.

It would be so easy for you to become like them, cared for and loved.

DEKKA: She's soft . . .

DAVA: . . . in the heed.

OLD LADY: Hard. Hard with years. I can see more of the city enclosed in this room than you will ever find loose around the streets. Look at these pictures collected over generations. Here you can see the passion of a city's people. The endless speculation. The pitiless exploitation. The smooth lipped politicians. Here is the market 50 years ago. The fixers. The grafters. Here are the councillors of my father's day, grand in their frock coats and whiskers and Bible-thumping morality. 'The rich man in his castle, the poor man at his gate' presented as the unalterable law of God. And no man can challenge God's law unless he has enough money.

DEKKA: She's mad.

DAVA: Loony.

OLD LADY: And what are you? You are the exploited children of confused, oppressed, skiving fathers, dulled with brown ale and aggressive sexuality. Why go back to be the stunted fathers of succeeding generations? Escape now while you have the chance. Find a universe in a room. Let each memory, each picture become an infinite window. (*She approaches them with a large pair of scissors.*) I have made children from rags before. They are craving for you. What can I not make from hot-blooded, breathing, ragged children?

DEKKA: Christ. Let's get out.

DAVA: Get out of our way.

They push the OLD LADY over. She screams and falls on her scissors. The boys try to help her and get blood on their hands.

DAVA: Dekka . . . I think she's deed.

DEKKA: Let's get out . . .

DAVA: We've killed her.

DEKKA: Let her be.

DAVA: Poor old cow.

They exit.

DEKKA *and* DAVA *stand in front of* SUPERINTENDENT INSPECTOR MURK *as they did in the opening scene.*

DAVA: We never killed her. She fell.

DEKKA: She was a witch.

MURK: There was a time when we used to hang young criminals like you in the market place . . .

DAVA: And burn witches, an'all.

MURK: Shut it! However, even the police force has to keep up with the times. You are going to be recycled instead. I'm going to see to it that you are both made safe. The urban comprehensive school has been one of the most effective innovations of recent years for ensuring the stupidity of the present generation, but you seem to have retained some degree of childish curiosity that might be hazardous. You are going to be put away. You will pass through the courts and experience the special training that will punish young killers like you in the way you deserve. You will, in fact, be subjected to a social lobotomy that will render what is left of your stunted imaginations to the consistency of ginger bread. In the far future, you will be dull enough to return home where you will find your parents old and white haired. They will scarcely recognise you. Meanwhile your father travels into work each day, his face grey and his eyes empty, and your mother weeps as she sweeps the laundrette floor.

DEKKA: There are more like us.

MURK: We will find them.

The cat mews.

DAVA: Not all of them.

The cat growls.

MIDNIGHT FEAST

Midnight Feast was commissioned by Scottish Television for their Preview series, and recorded in June 1982 with the following cast:

STEVENS   Robert Addie   } *Sixth form boys at Lochside Academy, Scotland*
STRAUN   Ian Michie

Directed by Hal Duncan
Designed by Paul Laugier
Produced by Robert Love

All characters and the school are fictitious.

It is past 11.30 at night at Lochside Academy, an independent boarding school for boys in the Highlands of Scotland.

The study of the housemaster, MR GEORGE 'TATTY' TAY, *is empty and dark.*

Two boys enter with torches. They are wearing pyjamas, dressing gowns and slippers.

STRAUN *checks that the curtains are securely drawn.*

STEVENS: Lights on, I think.

STRAUN: Are you sure?

STEVENS: Don't be common.

STRAUN *turns on the table lamp on the* HOUSEMASTER's *desk.*

STRAUN: Beaky was asleep?

STEVENS: Sounded like it.

STRAUN: Good.

STEVENS: Now where does our foolish housemaster keep his best glasses?

STRAUN: God! I need a drink.

STEVENS: You're such a plop, Straun.

STRAUN *finds some cut glass tumblers in a cabinet. He takes two out and pretends to throw one across to* STEVENS.

STRAUN: Catch!

STEVENS: Behave.

STRAUN *drops one of the glasses. It breaks.*

STEVENS: Terrific.

STRAUN: Do you think Tatty would like a new set of whisky glasses?

STEVENS *takes a bottle of whisky out of the* HOUSEMASTER's *drinks cupboard.*

STEVENS: You cause so much trouble, Straun.

STRAUN: I like ice.

STEVENS: How plebian.

STEVENS *pours two large whiskies. He settles down in the* HOUSEMASTER's *chair behind the desk.*

STRAUN: Don't you want some water?

STEVENS: You lack style, Straun.

STRAUN *is about to leave the room.*

Where are you going?

STRAUN: Ice.

STEVENS: Sit down, you dreg.

STRAUN *sits in front of the desk.*

STEVENS (*imitating* TATTY): You've been an absolute wreck this term, Straun. Untidy . . . frequently late for chapel . . . setting a lousy example to the junior boys. You've spent half your life on fatigues. Last week you played appallingly in the vital senior league match against MacLellan's.

STRAUN: Sorry, Sir.

STEVENS: You've been letting the whole side down in the most atrocious manner. I should beat you! I'd like to beat you! But I'm not going to . . . this time. Instead . . . cheers . . .

He raises his glass.

STRAUN: Cheers, Stevens.

They drink.

STEVENS: What's the time?

STRAUN: Twenty to midnight.

STEVENS: How splendid!

STRAUN: What shall we do with the broken glass?

STEVENS: We?

STRAUN: I mean . . . what shall I do with it?

STEVENS: Clear it up, I should think. It's your mess.

STRAUN: Thanks.

STEVENS: Oh God! God! God! Why doesn't he go to Edinburgh every night? How tolerable life would become. Tedium all day, followed by blissful nights.

STRAUN: We could always break out of bounds after lights.

STEVENS: Second year stuff! We should devote ourselves to pleasure and excitement. Drinking whisky in the bog, or climbing through windows in the dark and taking to the wild moors isn't my idea of fun. I therefore propose a toast to PLEASURE AND EXCITEMENT!

They drink.

It's the smells of this rotten school that depress me. Haven't you ever noticed, Straun, even with your minimal powers of observation, that when you come through to Tatty's side of the house ... the PRIVATE SIDE ... how the whole smell of the place changes? We spend most of our lives at Lochside Academy suffocating under the stench of hot boy ... sweaty boy ... pustular boy. Thompson's feet would revolutionise NATO's concepts of germ warfare. And God knows what it is that oozes from Walton major's crotch five times a day. But take a deep breath here, in our housemaster's inner sanctum, and find out how refreshing a few mildewed books and a hint of stale tobacco can be.

STRAUN: How long should we stay?

STEVENS: Cold feet now, is it?

STRAUN: No!

STEVENS: Our guardian for tonight, Beaky the Beast, had Horlicks with Maggot the Matron at ten thirty. Then, showing remarkable judgement, Old Beaky sneaked off to the Assistant Housemaster's humble hole on the junior floor. There he will get high on 'The Financial World Tonight' and end his day with a quick blast of 'Ere We Sleep.' Oh God! The TEDIUM!

STRAUN: I need ice.

STRAUN *creeps out of the study with his torch to look for ice in the kitchen.* STEVENS *tops up the glasses. There's a clatter offstage as* STRAUN *drops ice cubes all over the kitchen floor.*

STEVENS: Bastard!

STRAUN *gathers up the cubes he can find and carries a handful back to the study.*

STEVENS: Got what you wanted?

STRAUN: Sorry, Stevens. There are ice cubes all over the kitchen floor! Want some?

STEVENS: Good God no!

STRAUN: I found some cheese.

STEVENS: Excellent!

STRAUN *pulls a lump of cheese out of his dressing gown pocket and puts it on the* HOUSEMASTER's *desk, messily.*

STEVENS: You have a wonderful way with food, Straun.

STRAUN *tucks into the cheese, puts some of the ice in his drink, and places the rest of the ice cubes in an ashtray that he wipes clean on the curtain.*

STRAUN: Why did we wait four and a half years?

STEVENS: We? Why did I! It was me that dragged you along to this delectable little night spot. If I hadn't guided you from the dreary straight path, you'd be tucked up in bed dreaming of pillow fights unfought.

STRAUN: I propose a toast!

STEVENS: Really?

STRAUN: PILLOW FIGHTS!

STEVENS: Oh well ...

They drink.

Now I'm going to reveal to you an amazing fact.

STRAUN: I doubt it.

STEVENS: Straun, we don't have to be here!

STRAUN: That is truly amazing.

STEVENS: We don't have to be here.

STRAUN: No.

STEVENS: We hate this place, but we stay. We hate its dullness, the way it strangles originality out of our lives. We hate its structures, its rules, its outrageous hierarchy that turns boy against boy and which favours every nasty little opportunist. Why do we stay?

STRAUN: To take our exams.

STEVENS: It's a trap. Our exams are a trap. The prospect of university is a trap. We don't have to put up with it. We're both over school leaving age. We can walk out of here tonight and there's no one who could do a thing about it.

STRAUN: It's a long walk, Stevens.

STEVENS: I have a plan.

STRAUN: Yes.

STEVENS: Are you ready?

STRAUN: Would you like some more cheese?

STEVENS: Let's wait till Tatty gets back from Edinburgh.

STRAUN: You're crazy, Stevens!

STEVENS: Let's confront him tonight. We've had enough of Lochside.

STRAUN: He'd have us up and down that bloody mountain.

STEVENS: We should refuse.

STRAUN: My parents are coming up to take me out next weekend.

STEVENS: Let's save them the trouble.

STRAUN: They've spent thousands on me. I'm their pet project.

STEVENS: It would be wonderfully liberating.

He tops up the glasses.

Your family has betrayed you.

STRAUN: How?

STEVENS: They haven't been making huge sacrifices for your benefit. Your father's rolling in it anyway.

STRAUN: Hardly.

STEVENS: They've sold you into the slavery of this dreadful school to satisfy their own ambitions. Your life is just an extension of theirs. They sent you here. Remember? You never had any choice in the matter.

STRAUN: I'm unconvinced, Stevens. We both have conditional places at universities. London University seems like an oasis after five years in the middle of nowhere.

STEVENS: Walking out doesn't mean that we would lose our chance of university.

STRAUN: It wouldn't help.

STEVENS: It probably wouldn't help. I agree.

STRAUN: When is Tatty likely to get back from Edinburgh?

STEVENS: My spy network informs me that he had two tickets for the Usher Hall concert. That ends at about twenty

to ten. Then he is inclined to stuff himself with expensive spaghetti. Assuming there are no delays on the road, I calculate that he'll be back between half past twelve and one.

STRAUN: Let's not push our luck.

STEVENS: You're an appalling coward, Straun. I always remember how you surrendered to a platoon from Murdoch's on Field Day during your first year.

STRAUN: I was outnumbered 50 to 1.

STEVENS: There were extenuating circumstances, but it was generally agreed that you lacked fighting spirit.

STRAUN: I'm not waiting up for Tatty. But don't let me stop you.

STEVENS: What a traitorous rat you are.

STRAUN: Anyway, I have another suggestion.

STEVENS: Speak.

STRAUN: Tatty keeps files on every boy in the house in that cabinet.

STEVENS: It's locked.

STRAUN: I know where he keeps the key.

STEVENS: Where?

STRAUN opens a drawer and produces a small key. He goes over to the filing cabinet, opens it, searches around in it and produces two files.

STRAUN: That's yours.

He gives it to STEVENS.

And this is mine.

STEVENS: Wait! I'll read yours and you read mine.

STRAUN: If you like.

They swap files and start to read them.

STEVENS: What a sickly child you were.

STRAUN: Was I?

STEVENS: I didn't know you broke your arm at prep school.

STRAUN: It got caught in the serving hatch during Sunday lunch.

STEVENS: I'm not surprised.

STRAUN: Listen to this, Stevens. This is Tatty's letter to the admissions tutor at

Edinburgh University.

'He has always been something of an individualist, sometimes to the profound irritation of those around him . . .'

True!

'He can be stubborn to the point of selfishness . . .'

STEVENS: That man needs a poke on the nose.

STRAUN: Hang on!

'. . . and his verbal exchanges with members of staff have been known to cause great resentment.'

STEVENS: Good!

STRAUN: 'However, no one here doubts his ability as a scholar . . .'

I do. It's me that unscrambles your Latin Unseens.

'. . . but he has always been unwilling to contribute to the team spirit of the House.'

I think you got off rather lightly.

STEVENS: It seems I have achieved something.

STRAUN: I'm amazed they even offered you a provisional place.

STEVENS: Tatty's got a damned cheek, writing that stuff behind my back.

STRAUN: He's rather gone up in my estimation.

STEVENS (*reading*): 'He started out as a sweet-natured boy, always keen to lend a helping hand . . .'

STRAUN: Rot!

STEVENS: '. . . and he has distinguished himself each year in the House Play Competition.'

Nasty little show off!

STRAUN: Are you making that up?

STEVENS: No, you sweet-natured boy. It's all here.

STRAUN: Oh God!

STEVENS: 'However . . .'

Tatty's got the knife out now, even for you, Straun.

'. . . during the last year, he has been something of a problem, and I must

report that he turned down the opportunity of becoming a House Prefect, the only boy to do so in my entire experience as a housemaster.'

Something for which I admire you enormously, Straun.

STRAUN: Thank you.

STEVENS: Unfortunately he never gave me the chance of being the second boy in his entire experience to do so. There is something profoundly sad about these letters. They are obituaries. After four and a half years, in which we have grown from squeaky little children in short trousers into something purporting to be adulthood, that man, who has ruled and structured our lives, dispenses his assessment of us on less than a side of paper. I don't recognise you from this, Straun. He doesn't know either of us at all. And the greatest presumption, the greatest arrogance of this school . . . and for all we know all other schools . . . is that THEY know what is best for US! Their ideals, their religion, their ethos are what our parents are trying to buy. I say now . . . let me live MY life in MY way, making MY mistakes. OUR LIVES, Straun!

STRAUN: Our lives.

They drink.

STEVENS: What's the time?

STRAUN: Just past midnight.

STEVENS: If he comes back before we've finished, let's become his problem.

STRAUN: I'm in no hurry.

STEVENS: Do you realise! We're expected to get up at 7 o'clock for PT.

STRAUN: The LONG sharp shock. I shall probably throw up.

STEVENS: You probably will.

He eats some of the cheese.

Ummmmm . . . this cheese isn't bad.

STRAUN: Don't hog it all!

STEVENS: Did he have anything else worthwhile in the kitchen?

STRAUN: The cupboard was depressingly bare.

STEVENS: I am tempted to change some

of your grades. I think your half termly B for French really should adjust itself to a B+. What do you think?

STRAUN: Are grades important? To hell with them. If Mouchoire wants to give me a B, that's his problem. I don't give a damn. Leave it, Stevens.

STEVENS *is looking for a pen.*

STEVENS: It appeals to me.

STRAUN: I said leave it!

STEVENS: OK.

STRAUN: What else is there in my file.

STEVENS: A letter from your prep school head. Sickeningly flattering. Various medical documents. An 'Emergency Operations' form.

STRAUN: You've got one of those.

STEVENS: Tatty has permission to have us cut up! Nothing else much. Copies of your reports.

STRAUN: I didn't know your father was in fact your step father.

STEVENS: What?

STRAUN: That's what it says here.

STEVENS: What?

STRAUN: It says . . . your father is in fact your step father . . .

STEVENS: Let me see.

STRAUN *hands him a letter from* STEVEN's *mother to the* HOUSEMASTER.

It's from my mother.

He reads it.

She says in her last paragraph that on no account am I to be told I was adopted!

STRAUN: I didn't read that far.

STEVENS: That's staggering.

STRAUN: Is it true?

STEVENS: I suppose it must be. Why didn't they tell me?

STRAUN: I don't know.

STEVENS: I suppose that's great news.

STRAUN: Is it?

STEVENS: I don't have to go through life wondering if I'm going to turn out like father. He's a silly old sod! God! What a reprieve.

STRAUN: We ought to drink to that.

STEVENS: Definitely.

STRAUN: SILLY OLD SODS!

STEVENS: SILLY OLD SODS!

They drink.

Do you think I need to be christened again? Or registered with the Scottish Tourist Board as an alien, or something?

STRAUN: I don't think you're legal tender, Stevens.

STEVENS: My God! I'm a bastard!

STRAUN: BASTARDS!

STEVENS: BASTARDS!

They drink.

STRAUN: Quite a good party this.

STEVENS: Not bad.

STRAUN: Let's take all the personal files to the dormitories and hand them round.

STEVENS: Do you know, Straun, I prefer you when you're slightly drunk. I wonder what other revelations lurk within.

STRAUN: I'm convinced that Millbank's father is a baboon.

STEVENS: Harrington definitely comes from outer space.

STRAUN *looks at his watch.*

STRAUN: I have often thought I was adopted.

STEVENS: You're not, though.

STRAUN: No. I'm sure I'm not. I can see both my parents in me. Looking at photographs of when they were my age, I can see parts of myself staring back. But I've still thought sometimes, can these people really be my parents? I'm jealous of you, Stevens.

STEVENS: Parents should only be encountered by consenting minors in private. Such embarrassment at parents' weekends!

STRAUN: I only go with them for the food.

STEVENS: They wear such appalling clothes, especially mothers. Mine never looks the way she does here at home.

STRAUN: It's the hats that get me.

STEVENS: And the phoney conversations. Being so sickeningly polite. Parents really undermine our credibility.

STRAUN: And the staff become even more repulsive than usual. The way they pretend they like us.

STEVENS: Beaky once thought my mother was Mrs Smith-Taylor!

STRAUN: Oh God!

STEVENS: Parents are the ultimate humiliation.

STRAUN: I've suggested to mine that instead of travelling all the way up here twice a term, they just send me the money.

STEVENS: Good idea.

STRAUN: Are you going to tell yours you've found out?

STEVENS: I don't know. What would you do?

STRAUN: I think I'd say nothing.

STEVENS: Why?

STRAUN: I could watch the way they lie. The whole thing's built on deception. Like this place. From now on, you can understand all the things they DON'T say to you.

STEVENS: And you're jealous.

STRAUN: Yes.

STEVENS: They've always made the most tremendous fuss of me. Quite overpowering. Something to escape from. They used to organise birthday parties. When I was young. Wretched little children would be invited. Most of them I couldn't stand. They weren't my friends. It was their party. I mean my mother and father. I was their front man. But the worst part of all was being forced to wear a deplorable bow tie. And having my hair all smarmed down by mother. But the bow tie was the worst. It only appeared once or twice a year. It was blue, speckled with white. There was always a great fight about it. I used to lose. There is something grotesque about children in bow ties.

STRAUN: But they have done you a good turn.

STEVENS: Depends how you want to look at it.

STRAUN: You might still be in a children's home.

STEVENS: I'm a bit old for that now.

STRAUN: Or in care. Some sort of hostel.

STEVENS: What would you call this place?

STRAUN: What has kept you here all this time?

STEVENS: The fog has been slow in clearing. How are you supposed to know about things ... I mean what's happening outside of our lives ... when there's so little contact, so little first-hand experience to make decisions by? Why haven't you left?

STRAUN: Things are neatly parcelled up the way they are. I mean the timing of things. Exams in a few months. Then the summer holidays. Then, with a bit of luck, three years at university. I know what's happening. I don't like all of it, but at least it's clearly structured. If I suddenly say 'to hell with it all', the future becomes one big blank.

STEVENS: Exciting.

STRAUN: Which is more frightening? What you know? Or what you don't know?

STEVENS: I don't think of things in terms of fear. I'm thinking of freedom of choice.

STRAUN: I think we should destroy our files. Tatty has no right to know things we don't.

STEVENS: We should be selective about it.

STRAUN: OK. It's not unreasonable for him to have some of this stuff. It's the private letters ... the secret reports. Let's get rid of them for a start.

STRAUN *takes his own file and gives* STEVENS *his. They start removing letters and other material that seems to be private and personal from their files.*

STEVENS: We'll leave this stuff our parents filled in.

STRAUN: Right. I think there's a case for the 'Emergency Operations' form.

STEVENS: Letters from previous headmasters are out.

STRAUN: I don't know. Mine's quite flattering.

STEVENS: Not the point!

STRAUN: If yours said you were some sort of hero, you'd want to leave it in.

STEVENS: It's behind our backs, isn't it! Whatever it says.

STRAUN: Shouldn't we work the system to our advantage?

STEVENS: You're not pure.

STRAUN: No.

STEVENS: Give me that!

STEVENS *grabs the letter from STRAUN's old headmaster.*

STRAUN: Grow up, Stevens.

STEVENS: You're just reaffirming that you're a nasty little creep!

STRAUN: This is about rights, Stevens. My right to have in my file what I want.

STEVENS *tears up the letter in the most tantalising fashion.*

STRAUN: Bastard!

STEVENS *throws all the bits of paper at STRAUN.*

STEVENS: You can have your bloody letter!

STRAUN *takes the whole of STEVEN's file and tears it into shreds. When STEVENS sees what STRAUN is doing, he grabs the rest of STRAUN's file and tears it up as well.*

STRAUN: Well done, Stevens!

STEVENS: I'd hate to spoil your evening.

STRAUN: You really like to get on top of people.

STEVENS: Given half a chance.

STRAUN: Pontificating . . .

STEVENS: Ooooooo . . . !

STRAUN: You're sick, Stevens!

STEVENS: Calm down, little boy.

STRAUN: And you're hogging the whisky.

STRAUN *takes the bottle and fills up the glasses.*

STRAUN: What a bloody mess!

STEVENS: Shut up and eat your cheese.

STRAUN *picks up the lump of cheese and throws it at STEVENS. It misses and knocks a vase off the mantlepiece. It falls and breaks.*

STEVENS: I think you've just won a coconut.

STRAUN: What a bloody shambles!

STEVENS: I thought we were straightening things out.

STRAUN: It's people like you that get vandalism a bad name.

STEVENS: You're smashing the place up.

STRAUN: You've driven me to it.

STEVENS: Have we reached the point of no return yet?

STRAUN: I'm going to bed soon.

STEVENS: Don't you think you should tidy up?

STRAUN: Can't be bothered.

STEVENS: Even a dimwit like Tatty might suspect something.

STRAUN: I don't care. I'd really like to give that man a bloody nose. That would be a wonderful end to the evening. I'm tired of being on the receiving end of every bloody thing! That includes you. God! You get on my wick sometimes!

STEVENS: I think the whisky's gone to your balls, Straun.

STRAUN: My God I hope so!

STEVENS: Stop being a weed.

STRAUN: I'm not a weed!

STEVENS: Another drink?

STRAUN: I'm going to be in charge. From now on!

STEVENS: The new Straun!

STRAUN: I'll amaze everyone!

STEVENS: You will.

STRAUN: Yes!

STEVENS: Are you tidying up?

STRAUN: Should we?

STEVENS: Let's sleep on in the morning.

STRAUN: Double French followed by double PT. Do you think they're training me for the Invasion of Normandy?

STEVENS: In my second year, as an innocent boy in the Combined Cadet Corps, I had a lecture on how to slit an enemy's throat, commando style, without him screaming.

STRAUN: Who by?

STEVENS: Boyle. A spotty lance corporal, now reading medicine at Kings College London. The only Old Lochsider ever to appear on University Challenge.

STRAUN: Every boy should learn at an early age how to murder silently. It provides them with a solid moral foundation on which to build their lives, I always think. Should we slit Tatty's throat?

STEVENS: Would he bleed enough to make it worthwhile?

STRAUN: I doubt it.

STEVENS: You're thinking along the right lines.

STRAUN: I think a few heads should start to roll.

STEVENS: Shall we do extra woodwork and build a guillotine?

STRAUN: Shall we leave a note? 'Sorry about the mess. Straun and Stevens.'

Sound of a car coming up the drive and stopping outside the house. STRAUN has turned out the light.

STEVENS: Don't panic!

STEVENS turns on the table lamp.

STRAUN: He'll see.

STEVENS: Dry up.

STRAUN: Turn it off!

STEVENS: I refuse to behave like a thief in the night.

Sound of a key in the front door and of someone entering the house. Footsteps in the central hall outside the study where the boys are.
The footsteps move off to the kitchen.

STEVENS (*quietly*):
TAAAAATTTTYYYYYYYYYY!
Where arrrrrrrrrre yooooooooo?

STRAUN: I'll kill you!

Sounds of activity in the kitchen. A sudden cry and a crash.

STEVENS: My God! He's trodden on one of your ice cubes!

The two boys are killing themselves with laughter, but trying not to make a noise.
Sounds of TATTY, possibly a bit drunk himself, picking himself up.

STEVENS: We really ought to help the poor soul.

STEVENS moves off towards the door. STRAUN pulls him back. Sounds of TATTY staggering off upstairs to bed. When everything is completely quiet, the boys start to relax.

STEVENS (*whispering*): I THINK WE SHOULD GO TO BED!

STRAUN (*whispering*): WE HAVEN'T FINISHED OUR DRINKS!

STEVENS (*singing quietly*): 'Oh what a beautiful evening . . .'

STRAUN: Wrap up, Stevens. I propose the last toast.

STEVENS (*imitating the Last Post*): Daaaaaa . . . Daaaaaaaaaaaaa! Daaaa . . . Daaaaaaaaaa!

STRAUN: The last TOAST, idiot!

They are laughing away, trying not to make too much noise.

STEVENS: The bitch might have told me.

STRAUN: What?

STEVENS: My mother. She might have done. What a bloody stupid secret. It's the lack of trust. I hate her for that.

STRAUN: I'm very sorry, Stevens.

STEVENS: You're a coward, Straun.

STRAUN: COWARDS!

STEVENS: COWARDS!

They drink their glasses dry.

STRAUN: Pick up the paper!

STEVENS: Do we have to?

*They pick up the pieces of torn up
paper etc. from their files and stuff the
bits into their dressing gown pockets.
    STRAUN picks up the bits of
broken glass and puts them onto the
desk next to the bits of cheese.*

STEVENS: Hurry up!

STRAUN: Don't panic, Stevens.

*STRAUN takes the glasses and wipes
them dry on the curtain. He then puts
them back in the cupboard. He then
gets his torch out and turns off the
table lamp. STEVENS is peering
through the half opened door, torch
in hand.*

STEVENS: Come on!

*STRAUN knocks over the table lamp,
but catches it before it hits the floor.
STEVEN's torch shows up the broken
glass and the remains of the cheese on
the table.*

STEVENS: Leave them there.

STRAUN: Something to remember us by.

*They creep back to their side of the
house.*

Further titles in the Methuen Modern Plays
are described on the following pages.

Barrie Keeffe	*Gimme Shelter (Gem, Gotcha, Getaway)*
	Barbarians (Killing Time, Abide With Me, In the City)
	A Mad World, My Masters
Arthur Kopit	*Indians*
	Wings
Larry Kramer	*The Normal Heart*
John McGrath	*The Cheviot, the Stag and the Black, Black Oil*
David Mamet	*Glengarry Glen Ross*
	American Buffalo
David Mercer	*After Haggerty*
	Cousin Vladimir and *Shooting the Chandelier*
	Duck Song
	The Monster of Karlovy Vary and *Then and Now*
	No Limits To Love
Arthur Miller	*The American Clock*
	The Archbishop's Ceiling
	Two-Way Mirror
	Danger: Memory!
Percy Mtwa	
Mbongeni Ngema	*Woza Albert!*
Barney Simon	
Peter Nichols	*Passion Play*
	Poppy
Joe Orton	*Loot*
	What the Butler Saw
	Funeral Games and *The Good and Faithful Servant*
	Entertaining Mr Sloane
	Up Against It
Louise Page	*Golden Girls*
Harold Pinter	*The Birthday Party*
	The Room and *The Dumb Waiter*
	The Caretaker
	A Slight Ache and other plays
	The Collection and *The Lover*

John Kirkmorris: *Coxcombe;* John
Peacock: *Attard in Retirement;* Olwen
Wymark: *The Child*)

Best Radio Plays of 1981 (Peter Barnes:
The Jumping Mimuses of Byzantium;
Don Haworth: *Talk of Love and War;*
Harold Pinter: *Family Voices;* David
Pownall: *Beef;* J P Rooney: *The Dead
Image;* Paul Thain: *The Biggest
Sandcastle in the World*)

Best Radio Plays of 1982 (Rhys
Adrian: *Watching the Plays Together;*
John Arden: *The Old Man Sleeps
Alone;* Harry Barton: *Hoopoe Day;*
Donald Chapman: *Invisible Writing;*
Tom Stoppard: *The Dog It Was
That Died;* William Trevor: *Autumn
Sunshine*)

Best Radio Plays of 1983 (Wally K Daly:
Time Slip; Shirley Gee: *Never in My
Lifetime;* Gerry Jones: *The Angels They
Grow Lonely;* Steve May: *No
Exceptions;* Martyn Read: *Scouting for
Boys*)

Best Radio Plays of 1984 (Stephen
Dunstone: *Who Is Sylvia?;* Don
Haworth: *Daybreak;* Robert Ferguson:
Transfigured Night; Caryl Phillips:
The Wasted Years; Christopher Russell:
Swimmer; Rose Tremain: *Temporary
Shelter*)

Best Radio Plays of 1985 (Rhys
Adrian: *Outpatient;* Barry
Collins: *King Canute;* Martin
Crimp: *The Attempted Acts;*
David Pownall: *Ploughboy
Monday;* James Saunders:
Menocchio; Michael Wall:
Hiroshima: The Movie)